The Church Beyond the Wall

The Church Beyond the Wall

Life and Ministry in the Former East Germany

JAMES S. CURRIE

WIPF & STOCK · Eugene, Oregon

THE CHURCH BEYOND THE WALL
Life and Ministry in the Former East Germany

Copyright © 2019 James S. Currie. All rights reserved. Except for brief quotations in critical publications or reviews, no part of this book may be reproduced in any manner without prior written permission from the publisher. Write: Permissions, Wipf and Stock Publishers, 199 W. 8th Ave., Suite 3, Eugene, OR 97401.

Wipf & Stock
An Imprint of Wipf and Stock Publishers
199 W. 8th Ave., Suite 3
Eugene, OR 97401

www.wipfandstock.com

PAPERBACK ISBN: 978-1-5326-5221-9
HARDCOVER ISBN: 978-1-5326-5222-6
EBOOK ISBN: 978-1-5326-5223-3

Manufactured in the U.S.A.   JANUARY 10, 2019

Contents

Preface | vii
Introduction | ix

Chapter 1: Understanding the Background | 1

Chapter 2: GDR Church Leaders | 13

Chapter 3: Barth, Bonhoeffer, and Hanfried Müller |19

Chapter 4: Müller's Language and Ideology | 43

Chapter 5: The Ministry and Theology of Johannes Hamel | 60

Chapter 6: Conclusion | 78

Bibliography | 81
Index | 89

Preface

IN MAY 1991 I traveled to Germany in search of a dissertation topic. I was particularly interested in the church in the former East Germany, or the German Democratic Republic (GDR), a country under Communist rule from 1949 to 1989. While in Halle, I had the privilege of meeting with Dr. Michael Beintker, professor of theology at the University of Halle. Professor Beintker was among those who spoke out against the regime and was acutely aware of the fact that his phone was tapped by government authorities and that he was under surveillance in other ways. Not long after our meeting in Halle, he went on to Münster in the former West Germany where he taught theology until his retirement.

In 1991, Beintker suggested that I look into the life and thought of one Hanfried Müller, a professor of theology at the Humboldt University in Berlin. Müller and his wife, Rosemarie Müller-Streisand, were unapologetic Marxist supporters of the East German regime. Indeed, Müller eagerly served as an informant for the government for 35 years. Müller also wrote one of the first published studies of the thought of Dietrich Bonhoeffer, *Von der Kirche zur Welt* in 1961. In addition to Bonhoeffer, Müller also claims to have been strongly influenced, in a positive way, by the work of Karl Barth. My dissertation sought to demonstrate a misappropriation of the thought of both Bonhoeffer and Barth, a misappropriation due, in large part, to Müller's prior commitment to Marxist ideology.[1]

---

1. The dissertation is titled "Christianity and Marxism: A Historical

Preface

Since the completion of the dissertation, I have become interested in the life of the larger church in East Germany, and particularly in the testimonies of both pastors and church leaders during the 40-year life of the GDR. The names of some of those persons are included in the pages that follow. In addition to their own words, I have been helped, among others, by such secondary works as Robert F. Goeckel's *The Lutheran Church and the East German State* (1990) and John P. Burgess' *The East German Church and the End of Communism* (1997).

In this study, however, I have chosen one particular person on whom to focus on, in contrast with Hanfried Müller, and that is Johannes Hamel. For most of Hamel's ministry, he served as a pastor to students at the University of Halle after World War II and as a lecturer in practical theology at the University of Naumburg from 1955 to 1976. I chose to look at Hamel because, in many ways, he reflected and tried to address the struggle many pastors must have felt as they sought to minister under difficult circumstances. I also chose Hamel because in his writings, speeches, and sermons he, like Müller, is clearly influenced by Barth, but his perspective contrasts sharply with that of Müller.

My aim is to demonstrate the importance of one's starting point in articulating the gospel. The argument here is that Müller's starting point is a commitment to Marxist ideology first and that that governs his theology, while Hamel's starting point is the gospel as articulated in Scripture. Their different points of departure make all the difference in the trajectories of their thought and convictions. A second aim is to reflect on how one lives out one's convictions in a land that is hostile to those convictions.

I am indebted to Professor Beintker for his suggestion to look at the work of Hanfried Müller in the first place, to Professor John Stroup of Rice University for his supervision of the original dissertation, and to my wife, Jo Ann, without whose encouragement and support this project would never have seen the light of day.

Perspective on the Role of Ideology in the Thought of Hanfried Müller." It was completed in 1997 at Rice University under the supervision of Professor John Stroup.

Introduction

IN NOVEMBER 1989, THE Berlin Wall came down. In addition to a new political and economic openness, albeit fraught with a new set of problems and frustrations, this event opened the door wider for outsiders to examine the church in East Germany and, more specifically, the life and theology of the church that developed over the 40 years of Communist-imposed isolation from the rest of the world.

While life in the former German Democratic Republic (GDR) was not an unknown quantity during this time, including to a certain extent the ecclesiastical and theological life, the opening of the Wall and the subsequent reunification of East Germany with the Federal Republic released and revealed, in greater completeness and complexity, voices and perspective which had heretofore been relegated to life behind the Iron Curtain.[1]

The non-violent revolution, or "Wende" as it is called, has revealed a theological and ecclesiastical world that struggled with establishing its integrity, independence, and acceptance in a totalitarian Communist state. There were churchmen and theologians who opposed the regime.[2] There were also some who sought to

---

1. See Besier and Wolf, "*Pfarrer, Christen und Katholiken.*"

2. E.g., on August 18, 1976, Oskar Bruesewitz, Lutheran pastor in Zeitz, committed suicide by self-immolation in a protest against both the policies of the state and the church. See Goeckel, *The Lutheran Church and the East German State*, 202, 239. Michael Beintker, professor of theology at the University of Halle, also opposed the regime and was under constant surveillance by the *Stasi*, the secret police. After 1989 he went on to join the faculty at the

INTRODUCTION

find a position of coexistence and mutual acceptance, if not respect.³ And there were some who embraced and supported the kind of ideology and socialism represented by the Communist state. Pastors had to decide how they would carry out their responsibilities without either succumbing to the dictates of governmental authorities or engaging in activities that might jeopardize their effectiveness as pastors.

After a historical overview of the development of the relationship between the church and the GDR, this book will first focus on Hanfried Müller, a professor of theology at the Humboldt University in East Berlin throughout the years of the GDR. As will be seen, Müller was an ardent Marxist and a strong supporter of the government. Indeed, so strong was his support that he voluntarily served as an informant for the *Stasi*, the East German secret police. He is of interest because of this apparent paradox of, on the one hand, being a Christian theologian, and on the other, actively engaging in activities on behalf of the government that seemed to oppose and suppress the church.⁴

The book will then turn to those pastors and churchmen who either opposed the East German government or tried to find ways to build a bridge that allowed the church to carry out its responsibilities without interference from the state. The names of some of these persons may be familiar, while others may not, but all sought to be engaged with the issue of faithfulness to the gospel of Jesus Christ in their own way. Some were more conservative, favoring policies identified with the western powers, while others, though more progressive, did not support the more repressive policies of the eastern powers. Most specifically, attention will be given to Johannes Hamel (1911–2002) and his ministry as seen primarily through two publications: *How to Serve God in a Marxist Land* (a

---

University of Münster in West Germany.

3. See especially Albrecht Schönherr, bishop of Berlin-Brandenburg during the early Honecker years and author of the conciliatory formula, "Kirche im Sozialismus" ("Church in Socialism").

4. None of Hanfried Müller's writings have been translated or published in English. Therefore, all translations of his writings in this book are by this author.

Introduction

conversation between Hamel and Karl Barth) and *A Christian in East Germany*, a collection of writings and presentations by Hamel.

One of the more fascinating aspects of the events of November 1989 is the role that the church played, not only in providing space for prayer services in the months leading up to November, but also in encouraging any and all protests be peaceful and nonviolent. Leipzig's Nikolaikirche was one of the centers of regular Monday evening prayer services. Christian Führer served as that church's pastor. Upon Führer's death on June 30, 2014, German President Joachim Gauck wrote, "Christian Führer was a bearer of hope to many people, both in his profession as a pastor and as one of the defining figures of the peace prayers in the Church of St. Nicholas as well as the Monday demonstrations in Leipzig that led to the peaceful revolution in East Germany."[5] Like Christian Führer, there were other pastors and church leaders who protested, peacefully, in a way that contributed to the downfall of the East German government.

The purpose of this book is to shed light on the various perspectives within the church during the 40 years of the German Democratic Republic. One of the questions that underlies this study is: does our theological point-of-view shape our political perspective, or does our political point-of-view shape our theological perspective? In other words, what is our starting point? By engaging in this study, I hope that this examination will lead many of us in the western church to reflect critically on our own system of government and our relationship to it. We are going through a time of deep division in this country, both politically and theologically. The roots of these divisions are as varied as they are deep. Perhaps this attempt to understand the situation elsewhere will help us understand our own.

---

5. David Henry, "Lutheran pastor, Christian Führer, East German dissident, dies at 71," *The Washington Post*, July 1, 2014.

CHAPTER 1

Understanding the Background

FOLLOWING THE DEFEAT OF Germany in World War II, the Allied powers (France, Britain, the United States, and the Soviet Union) divided Germany into four occupational zones and the city of Berlin into four sectors. This idea was discussed by Roosevelt, Churchill, and Stalin at Teheran in November 1943 and agreed upon by the same three leaders at Yalta in February 1945. Details were revised and refined by Truman, Churchill, and Stalin at Potsdam in the summer of 1945.

In July 1945, the Soviets insisted that the other three powers withdraw from the area designated for Soviet occupation. Terms of occupation as well as the issue of reparations were only two matters that led to early friction among the four powers and prevented any peace agreement. This deadlock laid the foundation for a divided Germany and the beginnings of the Cold War. While the Soviets socialized all industry and instituted radical agrarian reforms in their zone in the east, the three western powers cooperated in planning for democratic elections in the western zones.

Tensions escalated when, in March 1948, the Soviets attempted to prevent all access to Berlin by the Allied powers. The immediate causes were threefold: (a) the desire to halt introduction of western currency into Berlin, (b) objections to steps being taken in the west to form a government in the three western zones of occupation, and (c) the desire to make the entire city of Berlin a part of the Soviet-occupied territory. The Berlin blockade lasted until May 1949. The airlift of food and other supplies by the western powers prevented the realization of any of the Soviets' short-term goals. In that respect the blockade failed. Berlin had become the focal point, both literally and symbolically, of the Cold War.

The division between East and West Germany became solidified when the western powers instituted monetary reform in their zones of occupation, i.e., they established the German *deutsche mark* as the legitimate currency. The Soviet Union countered by instituting their own monetary reforms in the eastern zone. The division was formalized in 1949. Following a six-nation conference in London in the spring, the Federal Republic of Germany was proclaimed in Bonn on May 24, 1949. A parliamentary democracy would be the form of government and a Basic Law (*Grundgesetz*) was adopted (the word "constitution" was intentionally avoided, apparently, in recognition of the fact that Germany was divided and in the hope that this would not be a permanent division).

In response, on May 30, 1949 the Soviet representatives proclaimed the establishment of the German Democratic Republic with Berlin as its capital. In contrast to the Bonn government, in October 1949 a constitution was adopted in the East. In name, it was "democratic" and a "republic." In fact, it was based on the Soviet form of government.

For the first 22 years of the GDR, the central figure was Walter Ulbricht, the son of a tailor in Saxony. Several factors combined to make those early years of the GDR more difficult than they might otherwise have been: the imposition of war reparations by the Soviet Union, the Soviet requirement that the GDR purchase its coal from Siberia instead of from the west (which would have been cheaper), a shortage of food, and a planned economy (based on the Soviet model) which demanded output quotas. Nevertheless, the

East German economy proved to be fairly progressive in its early years.[1]

Although production quotas in various industries (e.g., steel, chemical, and energy) were consistently met in the early years of the GDR, the government continued to increase the quotas.

As a result, the labor force began to protest. In the face of these protests, Ulbricht sought to accommodate the labor unions. However, in July 1952, new production quotas were imposed and worker income was reduced. Failure to meet some of these quotas led to supervisors in government-owned factories being tried and found guilty of sabotaging the new production goals. Many began to flee to the west. By the end of 1952, nearly 15,000 farmers and families had fled. Consequently, food shortages developed.[2]

Flight led to more government threats which led to further flight. The crisis came to a head in the spring of 1953.[3] Disregarding advice to the contrary from Moscow, Ulbricht and his colleagues decided to take a hard line toward the workers, increasing the work quotas by 10 percent in May. Although Ulbricht did, finally, accede to Soviet demands that he soften his approach, the quota increase remained in place. On the morning of June 16, many construction workers in East Berlin laid down their tools. Others joined them and the crowd soon numbered 10,000 persons. They marched to the Council of Ministers' *Stadthaus* and demanded to speak with Ulbricht and Minister President Otto Grotewohl. An official appeared and offered an ambiguously-worded statement. Somewhat confused as to whether the quotas had been rescinded or not, the crowd dispersed.

Henry Ashby Turner describes what followed the next day, June 17:

> On the morning of June 17, many workers in East Berlin declined to take up their tools. Instead, they gathered at their places of employment, elected strike committees,

1. Turner, *Germany from Partition to Reunification*, 68–69.
2. Turner, *Germany from Partition to Reunification*, 74.
3. The events of the uprising are described in Turner, *Germany from Partition to Reunification*, 73–80.

and marched to the government district, where they took over the city hall and surrounded the headquarters of the regime with a mass of humanity. On the way into the city, they tore down the regime's ubiquitous propaganda posters and billboards. Through Western news broadcasts, workers elsewhere in the GDR learned of developments in East Berlin and joined the strike, which quickly spread to over 200 localities throughout the GDR, especially those where industrial workers were numerous.[4]

Calling for free elections and for Ulbricht and Grotewohl to resign, the demonstrators set fire to the headquarters of the political police in East Berlin. But because there was no coordinated leadership, the uprising had begun to die down when Soviet troops arrived. The next day the government was back in control.

The 1953 uprising is important for several reasons. First, both the economic demands and the handling of the uprising demonstrated the dependence of the Ulbricht government on the Soviet Union. While over the course of its life the GDR economy would prove to be among the strongest in the eastern bloc, clearly it, along with its eastern neighbors, depended on Moscow economically, politically, and militarily. Second, the flight of East Germans to the west would continue to varying degrees until finally, on August 13, 1961, Ulbricht erected a wall separating East and West Berlin. Many who fled were farmers who were responding to a policy of mass collectivization of farmland by the government. The result was severe food shortage. Third, the heavy-handed response of the government to the 1953 uprising had a chilling effect on anyone, including the church, who might wish to register a protest regarding governmental policy. In March of 1954, the Soviet Union officially declared the GDR to be a sovereign nation. In May of the following year, in response to the admission of West Germany to the North Atlantic Treaty Organization (NATO), East Germany was included as a charter member of the Warsaw Pact.[5]

---

4. Turner, *Germany from Partition to Reunification*, 76–77.
5. Turner, *The Two Germanies Since 1945*, 125–26.

Understanding the Background

In 1969 Willy Brandt, the former mayor of West Berlin, was elected as the first Social Democratic chancellor of the Federal Republic of Germany. Until then, the Christian Democratic Union chancellors (Konrad Adenauer, Ludwig Erhard, and Kurt Kiesinger) had maintained a distant, if not hostile, view of the GDR. With Brandt came a new policy of "detente" toward his eastern neighbors. This was marked by Brandt's March 1970 meeting with Willi Stoph, the chairman of the GDR council of Ministers, in Erfurt in East Germany, as well as Brandt's visit to Warsaw, Poland in December 1970.

In May 1971 Ulbricht was removed from power. His successor was Erich Honecker, a faithful Communist Party member who, in 1961, had had the immediate responsibility of erecting the Berlin Wall. Under Honecker, Willy Brandt's overtures were not reciprocated. Honecker sought to integrate the GDR even more into the Soviet bloc. However, in 1972 the Brandt government proposed (and both countries signed) a Basic Treaty which included mutual recognition as sovereign states. Until this treaty, only nineteen countries had given the GDR diplomatic recognition.[6] This new international status and prestige led to less hostile relations between the two Germanys, although by no means could one call those relations warm.

The 1970s and 1980s brought economic difficulties in the GDR; these difficulties included food, housing, and labor shortages. The relationship between East and West Germany alternated between chilly and thawed. In 1981, West German Chancellor Helmut Schmidt visited Erich Honecker in a suburb of East Berlin. That visit, while cordial, occurred while Russians were fighting Afghans. The Soviets had also installed missiles aimed at western Europe. In Poland the communist government was suppressing the Solidarity movement and imposing martial law, and any hope for improving relations between the superpowers lost momentum with the election of a new, conservative American president, Ronald Reagan, in 1980. And yet, economic relations between the

---

6. Turner identifies these countries only as "those of the Soviet block plus some in Africa and Asia" (*Germany from Partition to Reunification*, 194).

5

GDR and the FRG did intensify in the 1980s. Travel restrictions were eased, and in the fall of 1987 Erich Honecker travelled to Bonn, West Germany and met with Chancellor Helmut Kohl.[7]

The 1980s, however, also brought increased dissent and a growing peace movement in the GDR.[8] The occurrence of more openness of expression in the Soviet Union under Mikhail Gorbachev (known as *glasnost*) seemed only to encourage such tendencies in the eastern bloc, including East Germany. Tensions between the government and dissidents increased. One wondered if the growing desire for freedom of expression and movement would be met with the kind of force that was exhibited in 1953 in Berlin, or in 1956 in Hungary, or in 1968 in Prague. Demonstrations grew throughout 1988 and 1989. People fled on trains when border restrictions were lifted between the GDR and Czechoslovakia.[9]

In November 1989 tensions reached new heights. It was also in that month that the government-planned celebration of the GDR's 40th anniversary was to be observed. Soviet President Gorbachev had been invited to attend. The result was hardly what Honecker and his colleagues had expected. Turner writes:

> In his official speech Gorbachev made clear that the days of the monolithic Soviet bloc were over and that each country must work out its own policies. In informal utterances to the press and to crowds in the streets he indicated sympathy for those demanding reforms. In return, the crowds appealed to him to support reform of the GDR and accorded him spontaneous cheers denied to Honecker and the other SED leaders. Gorbachev's visit left East German dissidents bolstered by the belief that they need not fear a repetition of the Soviet repression of June 1953.[10]

7. Bark and Gress, *A History of West Germany*, 516.

8. Prayer meetings began being held in churches throughout East Germany in 1981. For a collection of prayers offered at such meetings in the Nicolaikirche in Leipzig during 1989, see Hänisch et al, *Dona nobis pacem*.

9. Bark and Gress, 588–613.

10. Turner, *Germany from Partition to Reunification*, 230. The SED refers to the official Communist Party in the GDR (Socialist Unity Party). There have

Understanding the Background

On Saturday, November 4, a million persons demonstrated in East Berlin for democracy. On November 6, several hundred thousand persons demonstrated for unrestricted travel and for free elections. On November 7, the GDR government resigned. On November 8, the Politbüro resigned. On Thursday, November 9, all East German and East Berlin borders were removed, and the Wall came down.[11]

With this brief overview of the history of the GDR, we have a glimpse of the political events and environment in which Hanfried Müller chose to live and work. But what of the ecclesiastical and theological environment?

In the structure of the GDR hierarchy, the Department of Church Questions of the Secretariat of the Central Committee was the government organ that oversaw the life and work of the church. Established in 1958, this body "communicated state policy and negotiated directly with the churches.[12] There were, however, other governmental agencies that oversaw various aspects of the church's life. For example, Robert Goeckel notes,

> [t]he Ministry of Health dealt with church hospitals and other service agency institutions; the Ministry of Higher and Technical Education was responsible for the theology sections at the state universities; the Ministry

---

been several accounts of the events surrounding the 1989 demonstrations and the subsequent "bloodless revolution." For a view of the events throughout eastern Europe, see the collection of New York Times articles in *The Collapse of Communism* (edited by Bernard Gwertzman and Michael T. Kaufman); Timothy Garton Ash's *The Magic Lantern: The Revolution of '89 Witnessed in Warsaw, Budapest, Berlin, and Prague*; and Niels Nielsen's *Revolutions in Eastern Europe*. For an account of the day-by-day events as they unfolded in Leipzig churches, see Hans-Jürgen Sievers' *Stundenbuch einer deutschen Revolution. Die Leipziger Kirchen im Oktober 1989*. For a sociological analysis of the participants in the Leipzig demonstrations and activities, see *Leipzig im Oktober* (edited by Jürgen Grabner, Christiane Heinze, and Detlef Pollack).

11. For a complete list of dates of significant events in the life of the German Democratic Republic, see Hermann Weber's *DDR. Grundriss der Geschichte, 1945-1990*. It must be said that the immediate fall of the GDR was due to the collapse of the economy. Ideological issues must be considered secondary.

12. Goeckel, *The Lutheran Church and the East German State*, 34.

of Construction affected construction of churches; and the Ministry of Culture oversaw church publications. The Ministry of the Interior also played a large role in the Kirchenpolitik, since relations with the churches on the local and district levels were handled by the respective deputy chairman of the interior. [. . .] Of course, the Ministry for State Security maintained a special oversight role vis-a-vis the church establishment and individual Christians.[13]

There was also a political party, the CDU (Christian Democratic Union), the main target group of which was Christians. This party served as a conduit through which the government could often communicate its policies to the church. Conversely, the CDU also served the state by trying to mobilize support for state policies, especially when the state wanted to undermine the church leadership.

Goeckel maintains that the government "had four basic tactics at its disposal in pursuit of its goals in the Kirchenpolitik: atheistic propaganda, political mobilization, administrative measures, and cadre policy."[14] Atheistic propaganda revolved around educational and mass media practices in the promotion of Marxism-Leninism. Political mobilization, designed to limit criticism of the state by the church, promoted political support and activity among Christians. Administrative measures consisted of constraints and rewards, depending on the political climate and the degree of cooperation of the church. Finally,

> [c]adre policy refers to the personnel files on individuals, which were used in decisions regarding educational and career advancement. These often contained information on the individual's participation in mass organizations and state activities, such as the youth dedication ceremony (or Jugendweihe), and even on participation in confirmationand church membership. By using this cadre policy to limit the advancement of individual Christians,

---

13. Goeckel, *The Lutheran Church and the East German State*, 35.
14. Goeckel, *The Lutheran Church and the East German State*, 38.

the state exerted pressure on the church adherence and political stance of individual Christians.[15]

In summarizing the structural relationship between the East German church and the state, Goeckel observes:

> The state faced a church that has historically been characterized by a decentralized yet democratic structure and by a theology that has stressed deference to the authority of the state. [...] The church in turn faced a Communist party guided by an ideology that both affirmed scientific atheism yet allowed a certain tactical flexibility. The church also confronted a strong state which, despite its rather liberal constitution, was armed with various levers of influence over the church and believers.[16]

For the first twenty years of the GDR, the Protestant church had maintained organizational ties to the Protestant church in West Germany. This caused a good deal of tension between state authorities and the church. This tension was exacerbated by the fact that the bishop of Berlin-Brandenburg from 1945 to 1966, Otto Dibelius, not only held ecclesiastical authority in both East and West Berlin, but was also staunchly anti-communist.

In 1969, however, the Protestant church acceded to the government's wishes and severed all formal ties with the church in West Germany. Informal ties remained through underground financial support from the west. Dibelius was succeeded by a more conciliatory bishop, Albrecht Schönherr, who had studied under Dietrich Bonhoeffer in 1935 at the Finkenwalde seminary.[17] While

---

15. Goeckel, *The Lutheran Church and the East German State*, 39. Ironically, the youth dedication ceremony (*Jugendweihe*) of the GDR has its roots in the similar practice of indoctrination in the Hitler Youth. For more information on that movement, see George L. Mosse's *The Crisis of German Ideology: Intellectual Origins of the Third Reich*, 171–89, and *Nazi Culture: Intellectual, Cultural and Social Life in the Third Reich*, 262–318.

16. Goeckel, *The Lutheran Church and the East German State*, 39.

17. In his biography of Dietrich Bonhoeffer, *Dietrich Bonhoeffer: Man of Vision, Man of Courage*, Eberhard Bethge mentions Schönherr's participation in the Finkenwalde seminary (see Bethge, *Dietrich Bonhoeffer*, 158, 358, 386, 422, 439–40, and 491).

not an enthusiast for the GDR regime, Schönherr demonstrated a willingness to work more cooperatively with the government. In 1971, he "held out an olive branch to the regime by proclaiming the clergy's readiness to serve as a 'church within socialism.'"[18] The state accepted this offer and, as a result, the church was able to achieve the right to participate in international conferences and enjoyed some degree of tolerance from the state, while the state obtained a pledge from the church to restrain its criticism of the state.

Despite the apparent growing rapprochement, within two or three years frustration in the church began to grow again. The sources were several: (a) the state's youth policy which limited the free time of young people; (b) discrimination in the education of church workers; and (c) the issue of the possibility of unarmed military service, or alternative forms of national service, for Christians.[19]

Some in the church became skeptical of Schönherr's policy of accommodation toward the state. This skepticism and frustration was graphically demonstrated in the town square of Zeitz by Oskar Bruesewitz, the local pastor, on August 18, 1976. Robert Goeckel describes the gruesome incident:

> After unrolling a banner that decried the ruination of the youth and proclaimed a battle between darkness and light, Bruesewitz doused himself with gasoline and set himself afire. He died four days later.[20]

The Bruesewitz suicide led to an unprecedented summit meeting on March 6, 1978 between Honecker, Schönherr, and the Executive Board of the Kirchenbund.[21] The concessions to which Honecker

---

18. Turner, *Germany from Partition to Reunification*, 199.
19. Goeckel, *The Lutheran Church and the East German State*, 236-37.
20. Goeckel, *The Lutheran Church and the East German State*, 239.
21. For an account of this summit meeting, see Goeckel, *The Lutheran Church and the East German State*, 241-46. Schönherr himself provides an account in an address delivered on February 10, 1986 before the Christian Democratic Union in Berlin. This address was reprinted and published in *Occasional Papers on Religion in Eastern Europe*: see Schönherr, "A Contribution

Understanding the Background

agreed included greater church access to East German television, greater access to imprisoned ministers, building new churches, including clergy and other church workers in the state's pension system, and assistance in facilitating church congresses. However, Goeckel notes,

> the primary import of the summit lay not in these concrete agreements and expanding international opportunities but rather in ratifying the basis of the new relationship between church and state that had developed since 1971 [. . .] It is important to underscore that the March 6 summit did not represent a concordat between church and state, nor did it produce a communique with binding character on the participants.[22]

During the next twelve years when political dissent increased, the church served "as both an umbrella for the expression of oppositional views and a channel for and domesticator of such views."[23] One interesting indication of the new relationship between the church and the GDR government occurred on the occasion of Martin Luther's 500th birthday in 1983. The government "not only revised its negative interpretation of Luther's role but also extended unprecedented assistance to the church in its celebration."[24] Unprecedented publicity accompanied plans for the celebration. Honecker himself chaired the official Martin Luther Committee of the GDR.

The church was somewhat ambivalent to this sudden enthusiasm by the state. Goeckel

> describes this ambivalence: It knew of Luther's negative side and the cloud over pre-1945 Luther anniversaries, which had been demonstrations of anti-Catholicism, German internationalism, and fascism. Many felt that the true needs of the church would be overlooked in

---

to the Direction of the Evangelical Church in the German Democratic Republic."

22. Goeckel, *The Lutheran Church and the East German State*, 243–44.
23. Goeckel, *The Lutheran Church and the East German State*, 247.
24. Goeckel, *The Lutheran Church and the East German State*, 248.

this euphoria and that the issues of contention with the state, such as discrimination and militarization of society, should be addressed. Yet the church could hardly ignore the international attention of world Lutheranism, and the increased contact between Marxist and church historians argued for cooperation with the state.[25]

Tensions arose with the state when the church leadership tried to exert some independence in planning the Luther celebration. In response to a more balanced view of Luther presented by the church's planning committee, in November 1982 the GDR decided to proclaim 1983 as Karl Marx Year.[26]

In 1987 Berlin celebrated its 750th anniversary. Again, the church was included in this celebration. In June of that year the church hosted a convention, "the first since the construction of the Berlin Wall."[27]

In the 1980s there was increased attention, especially within the church, to issues of peace and the environment. In 1982 the church employed the motif "Swords into Ploughshares." Although this biblical motif "had been the subject of a Soviet sculpture presented to the United Nations and had long been officially accepted in the GDR,"[28] the church was now using it to protest increased militarization of the GDR as well as of the Soviet-Afghan war. In addition, a grass roots peace movement began meeting in churches in the early 1980s. Prayer meetings began being held on Monday evenings in the Nicolaikirche in Leipzig as well as in other churches around the country.[29] It was out of these Monday evening gatherings in churches that the massive protests emerged in 1989 that immediately preceded the fall of the GDR. Now, we will turn to some of the church leaders in the GDR.

---

25. Goeckel, *The Lutheran Church and the East German State*, 249.
26. Goeckel, *The Lutheran Church and the East German State*, 249–50.
27. Goeckel, *The Lutheran Church and the East German State*, 250.
28. Goeckel, *The Lutheran Church and the East German State*, 262.
29. See the collection of prayers in Hänisch et al., *Dona nobis pacem*.

Chapter 2

GDR Church Leaders

WE NOW TURN TO some of the churchmen and theologians who played an important role in the life of the church in the GDR from 1949 to 1989. Who were those who, like Müller, were concerned with state policies toward the church, but who were not, as Müller was, sympathetic with the Marxist state?

Mention has already been made of Albrecht Schönherr. An early member of the Confessing Church, Schönherr was a student of Bonhoeffer at the underground seminary in Finkenwalde in the 1930s. He was ordained in 1936 and served a Confessing congregation in Brüssow until the outbreak of World War II. At the end of the war he was a prisoner of the British in a field hospital in Italy. In 1946 he was appointed dean of the district of Brandenburg. From 1951 to 1962 he served as director of the Brandenburg preachers' seminar. In 1958 he was also a co-founder of the Weißenseer Working Group (of which Hanfried Müller was a part). In 1967, he became the interim bishop of Berlin-Brandenburg, succeeding Kurt Scharf who adamantly opposed the Communist regime was refused re-entry into East Berlin from West Berlin by the East German authorities. Two years later Schönherr became the bishop of Berlin-Brandenburg. It was in that position that he sought to find a middle way for clergy and the church to exist and function within the context of a Communist regime. Reflecting the biblical phrase "being in the world but not of the world" (Rom 12:2), the term "church within socialism" was an attempt to satisfy both the state and the church. In 1978 the GDR president Erich Honecker agreed to meet with officials of the Protestant Federation of Churches in the GDR of which Schönherr was chair (1969–1981). This meeting amounted to a concession on the government's part of the legitimacy of the church. Out of this meeting came an agreement by Honecker, among other things, to let new churches be built and to allow churches limited access to radio and television. Schönherr died March 9, 2009 at the age of 97 years.[1]

Johannes Hamel (1911–2002) is perhaps best known as the author of *A Christian in East Germany* and co-author (with Karl Barth) of *How to Serve God in a Marxist Land*.[2] Following World War II, Hamel served as pastor to students at the University of Halle, and from 1955 until his retirement in 1976 as lecturer in practical theology in Naumburg. In the spring of 1953 he, along with 70 other churchmen, was imprisoned by the State Security (Stasi). We will look more closely at him in subsequent chapters.

Heino Falcke (b. 1929) studied in Berlin, Göttingen, and Basel, but earned his doctorate in the east at the University of Rostock. Active in the "Federation of Protestant Churches in the GDR," Falcke also served as dean at Erfurt. According to Goeckel, he was especially active in the environmental movement in the 1980s. In 1972 Falcke earned the displeasure of the state in an address to the Kirchenbund synod. Goeckel writes:

> In it he rejected the state's view that faith may provide the motivation but that socialism alone can provide the normative content for social action. But he also rejected an introverted, apolitical religion. To Falcke, Christians are freed by Christ to pursue *mündige Mitverantwortung* (mature co-responsibility). [. . .] Socialism exists under

---

1. See obituaries in *The Independent Online*, March 19, 2009 and *The Guardian*, April 2, 2009.

2. *A Christian in East Germany* (New York: Association Press, 1960); *How to Serve God in a Marxist Land* (New York: Association Press, 1959).

the promise of Christ, according to Falcke. As a result, even when disappointed, Christians "With engaged hope of an improved socialism" can remain active in society. While endorsing socialism in the Third World and distancing himself from liberal notions of pluralism, he addressed many taboo topics of GDR socialism. He discussed the existence of suffering in socialism, alienation in the workplace, and the pressure to perform. [. . .] [H]e called for greater openness and information in GDR society. He rejected *Abgrenzung* as an attempt to stabilize society internally by fostering distance from outsiders.[3]

State officials attempted to have Falcke's address stricken from the synod's records, but failed in this attempt. However, the state "discredited Falcke's advice on the improving of socialism as 'modernization of bourgeois positions with the help of revisionist vocabulary.'"[4]

In his book *The East German Church and the End of Communism,* John Burgess points to Falcke's notion of a "spiritual-moral crisis" that enveloped not only the Marxist-Leninist state but also the West as being a key theme in East German theological-political thought:

> Falcke located the roots of this crisis in the basic human experience of "anxiety," that is, people's insecurity and fearfulness about the value and worth of their lives. People turn to those "gods" that seem to promise power and security. In the modern world, people especially worship a scientific-technological rationality that promises power through knowledge and manipulation. Yet this very reliance on science and technology has led to the modern crisis. Humans use science and technology in ways that dominate nature and each other.

The only way out of this crisis, according to Falcke, was "a new kind of relationship with God, based on confession and repentance."[5]

---

3. Goeckel, *The Lutheran Church and the East German State,* 175.
4. Goeckel, *The Lutheran Church and the East German State,* 176.
5. Burgess, *The East German Church and the End of Communism,* 76–78.

Clearly, this perspective did not endear Falcke to the East German state.

Friedrich-Wilhelm Krummacher (1901-1974) was elected bishop of the Pomeranian Protestant Churches in 1954 and lived in Greifswald. He also served as chairman of the Eastern Conference of Churches from 1960 to 1968. During the mid-1960s dispute over whether or not institutional ties with the Protestant church in West Germany should be maintained, Krummacher drew the ire of the GDR state for his part in the drafting of what became known as the Fürstenwalde Declaration. Goeckel summarizes the contents of this declaration:

> First, it maintained that separation from the EKD [Protestant Church of Germany] was required only in the case of false teaching or disobedience to God, which was not the case in the EKD. Second, the declaration maintained that there were good reasons to maintain organizational unity: the churches' guilt in the Third Reich, acknowledged in the Stuttgart Confession of 1945, and responsibility toward history and the German people in this regard; the imperative of the ecumenical movement; and the need to uphold human contacts between the two Germanies.[6]

Goeckel goes on to observe that Krummacher was openly charged in the Communist Party newspaper *Neues Deutschland* with being used by the West German "military church." Krummacher retired in 1972 and died in 1974.

Werner Krusche (1917-2009) became bishop of Saxony in 1968 and remained in that position until his retirement in 1983. Although he was raised in the east, Krusche was educated in the west (Heidelberg, Göttingen, Basel). He returned to East Germany in 1953 because of a shortage of pastors there. During the period 1969-1971, Goeckel notes, Krusche was viewed by the state as "the most threatening" churchman. This was largely due to Krusche's unwillingness to accept the state uncritically. According to Goeckel, he was willing to accept socialism in order to change it:

---

6. Burgess, *The East German Church and the End of Communism*, 67.

Although he accepted the socioeconomic basis of socialism, Krusche saw the churches' role in terms of cooperating to improve the "real existing socialism" along the lines of a democratic socialism. For example, he criticized the lack of free elections and argued for greater democratic freedoms.[7]

In 1990, a collection of Krusche's sermons from the 1980s was published under the title *Und Gott redete mit seinem Volk*. These sermons reflect Krusche's boldness in his critique of the state.

Gottfried Noth (1905-1971) became bishop of Saxony in 1953. With the exception of a time in Erlangen, his theological education took place in the eastern part of Germany. His pastorates were, for the most part, in or around Dresden. From 1954-1971 Noth was a member of the Central Committee of the World Council of Churches, and he attended the WCC conference in Evanston and New Delhi.[8]

Noth's participation in international ecumenical activities inevitably involved him in governmental skirmishes due to the GDR's skepticism about international contacts by its citizens. On the other hand, participation in international events by GDR citizens did provide prestige and credibility to the GDR state. Tension over this issue arose in the late 1960s when the government wanted the church to dissolve its institutional relationship with the church in West Germany and establish its own independent identity. Goeckel describes an event that occurred in 1969 which reflects both the ambivalence of the state in such matters as well as the friction between the church and the state:

> In November 1969 the WCC [World Council of Churches] invited representatives of the Kirchenbund to Geneva to negotiate the termination of the EKD's responsibility for the representation of the eight GDR churches and the transfer of this responsibility to the Kirchenbund. A delegation composed of Chairman Schönherr, Deputy Chairman Noth, and President Bräcklin was scheduled to

---

7. Burgess, *The East German Church and the End of Communism*, 143.
8. Besier and Wolf, "Pfarrer, Christen und Katholiken," 841.

travel in December 1969, but the visit was canceled at the last minute when the state refused a visa to Bishop Noth. Although Noth was no longer a member of the EKD Council, he remained barred from travel by the state for domestic political reasons: the incarceration of his son for aiding an escape attempt, Noth's bitter criticism of the state's harsh three-and-one-half-year sentence, and Noth's uncompromising opposition to the youth dedication ceremony and other policies of the GDR. Thus, the GDR, seeking to foster its international standing without sacrificing the goals of its domestic Kirchenpolitik, granted visas to only Schönherr and Bräcklin.[9]

While the ministry of all of these pastors and scholars are worthy of attention, particular heed will be given to that of Johannes Hamel, in part because he represents something of the experience of many pastors and scholars who resisted the East German government, and in part because the two volumes he authored and co-authored reflect explicitly the struggle of living and working as a Christian in a Marxist country. But first we will turn to the life and work of a very different perspective as represented by Hanfried Müller, a professor of theology who embraced Marxism and fully supported the East German government.

9. Goeckel, *The Lutheran Church and the East German State*, 120–21.

Chapter 3

Barth, Bonhoeffer, and Hanfried Müller

ARGUABLY, THE TWO MOST influential twentieth-century theologians in Protestant and Catholic circles were Karl Barth and Dietrich Bonhoeffer. Remarkably, together, their influence has not only spanned most of the century, but has also held fast during, and even transcended, the revolutionary political changes that took place between 1920 and 1990.

It is fair to say that the thought of Barth and Bonhoeffer had a profound impact on the church in the communist world of eastern Europe following World War II. Clearly, this was the case among theologians and the church in the German Democratic Republic, including one Hanfried Müller. This impact was due both to the depth of their theological insights and, equally important, to their interest and involvement in the social and political movements of the day. Therefore, as we consider the thought of Müller, it is appropriate and essential to do so in light of the influence of these two prominent theologians.

In September 1919, a conference on religion and social issues was held in Tambach, Germany. The historian, Klaus

Scholder, quotes Georg Merz's recollection of the participants in this conference:

> Those who met in Tambach came together more or less by chance. They belonged to none of the major, influential schools of thought, inclined to no political party, heeded the word of no leader. If they were united in one point it was that they wanted "something else." Because they suspected rather than knew that the social question was the problem of the time, they devoted themselves to questions which arose out of this problem and asked themselves about the position of Christians in church, state and society. Because they had heard of the Religious Socialist Movement in Switzerland, and because the names of Hermann Kutter and Leonhard Ragaz were familiar to them in this context, they invited these leaders to the conference.[1]

However, both Kutter and Ragaz, the founders and early leaders of the religious socialist movement in Switzerland,[2] declined in-

---

1. Scholder, *The Churches and the Third Reich*, 40.

2. For a brief introduction to the thought of Ragaz, see Pasztor, "Leonard Ragaz: Pioneer Social Theologian." For a helpful introduction to Christian socialism in Germany, especially the contribution of Adolf Stoecker, see Massanari, "Christian Socialism in Nineteenth Century Germany: A Case Study of a Shift in Anthropological Perspective."

It should be noted that there are many strands in the history of Christian, or religious, socialism. Stoecker, for example, was concerned about economic and social inequities, but he was also a nationalist and an anti-Semite. Ragaz, on the other hand, held a more internationalist perspective in his concern for the poor of the world. What these various views have in common is a tendency toward a communitarian perspective and away from pious individualism.

For a comprehensive treatment of religious socialism in Weimar Germany, including a comparison of Paul Tillich and Karl Barth in this regard, see Breipohl, *Religiöser Sozialismus Weimarer Republik*.

Also, during the Weimar years there appeared a publication, *Zwischen den Zeiten*, that held importance for a young group of theologians who not only subscribed to dialectical theology, but who also had been influenced by, and were sympathetic with, Christian socialism. Appearing from 1923 to 1933, it was published by Georg Merz and edited by Karl Barth, Friedrich Gogarten, and Eduard Thurneysen. Over the span of its life several articles on socialism and Christianity appeared as well as on church and state. For example,

vitations from the two organizers of the conference, Otto Herpel and Heinrich Schultheis, two pastors from Hesse.[3] Instead, Karl Barth, a young Swiss pastor who was unknown in Germany, was suggested as a possible speaker. Barth was asked to give the final address at this conference and he accepted the invitation.

In spite of Merz's characterization of the participants as having no commitments to a political ideology, party, or leader, it seems that they had certain hopes and expectations for this conference. Scholder notes that Günther Dehn, the center of a later controversy in Germany which also involved Karl Barth, "is surely right in thinking that those who were at Tambach expected something quite specific from Barth, namely, 'a sharp rejection of the capitalist economic and social order that was still in control [. . .] and an urgent challenge to contribute vigorously to the coming new socialist order.'"[4] It should be added that these expectations were not only influenced in part by the experience of World War I, but also by the ill-fated attempt at a revolution by Communists which began in a naval shipyard in Kiel in November 1918; the latter event was seen by many as a sign of hope for radical social and economic change.

Barth's lecture, "The Christian's Place in Society,"[5] while causing disappointment and consternation among those present, in Scholder's view, "belongs with Karl Holl's 1917 speech on Luther and Rudolf Bultmann's 1941 lecture on demythologizing as one of the most important testimonies of twentieth-century Protestant theology."[6] In this lecture Barth attacked the liberal theology of the nineteenth and early twentieth centuries on which he had

---

see "Sozialismus und Christentum" by Thurneysen in the first issue in 1923; "Hermann Kutter" by Thurneysen in the fourth issue of 1923; "Christentum und Marxismus" by Fritz Lieb in a 1929 issue; "Staat und Kirche" by Friedrich Gogarten in a 1932 issue; "Konfessionalität und politische Haltung" by Hans Asmussen in a 1933 issue; and "Theologisch-politischer Diskurs" by Hinrich Knittermeyer in the same 1933 issue.

3. Busch, *Karl Barth*, 109.
4. Scholder, *The Churches and the Third Reich*, 40.
5. Barth, *The Word of God and the Word of Man*, 272-327.
6. Scholder, *The Churches and the Third Reich*, 40.

been reared. He set in sharp distinction human society, however it may be organized and however noble its aims may be stated, from God and his kingdom: "The kingdom of God does not begin with our movements of protest. It is the revolution which is before all revolutions, as it is before the whole prevailing order of things."[7] While arguing that protest against the prevailing order of things may indeed be part of the kingdom of God, Barth warns against identifying any particular ideology, be it conservative or revolutionary, with the kingdom of God. Such an identification would amount to a betrayal of Christ:

> Today for the sake of social democracy, or pacifism, or the youth movement, or something of the sort—as yesterday it would have been for the sake of liberal culture or our countries, Switzerland or Germany—we may very well succeed, if the worst comes to the worst, in *secularizing* Christ. But the thing is hateful to us, is it not? We do not wish to betray him another time.[8]

The temptation to identify human causes with God's cause or kingdom is a dangerous one, according to Barth, because the two are quite different: Clever enough is the paradox that the service of God is or must become the service of man, but that is not the same as saying that our precipitate service of man, even when it is undertaken in the name of the purest love, becomes by that happy fact the service of God.[9]

Barth himself, no doubt, sympathized with the political views of many of those in his audience. After all, as pastor in Safenwil he had helped organize factory workers there and had antagonized industrial management by his actions and much of what he said. Among some he became known as "the red pastor." Indeed, in 1911 he presented a lecture with the title "Jesus Christ and the Social Movement." But the Tambach lecture reflected not only the new direction Barth's own theology had taken and would follow, in general, for the rest of his life, but it also reflected a challenge

---

7. Barth, *The Word of God and the Word of Man*, 299.
8. Barth, *The Word of God and the Word of Man*, 277.
9. Barth, *The Word of God and the Word of Man*, 276.

even to those with whose political views he may well have agreed. Eberhard Busch, Barth's biographer, notes that this lecture

> was so to speak a farewell to a theology which Barth himself had followed for sometime, and especially to Religious Socialism. [. . .] At the same time, however, the lecture also announced a new programme: one can say that it contains in germ ideas which Barth was then to develop in detail in subsequent years.[10]

Barth's interest in the relationship between church and society and between church and state continued throughout the rest of his life. He was the principal author of the Theological Declaration of Barmen, which articulated the Confessing Church's position regarding the relationship between church and state, and which represented its resistance to Hitler's demand for absolute obedience from the church. At various points in his *Church Dogmatics* as well as in separate letters, articles, and books, Barth continued to address this issue,[11] although it must be added that his interest was always in the context of his larger theological perspective.[12]

Similarly, Dietrich Bonhoeffer's influence came about in response to his experience with and involvement in the political world and events of his day. In the letters he wrote during the last year of his imprisonment, beginning in April 1944, Bonhoeffer began a new direction in his theological thought from that which he had developed in his earlier writings such as *Sanctorum Communio* (1927), *Act and Being* (1930), *Creation and Fall* (1933), *The Cost of Discipleship* (1937), *Life Together* (1938), and his incomplete writings on ethics.

---

10. Busch, *Karl Barth*, 111.

11. E.g., *Church and State*; *Against the Stream: Shorter Post-War Writings, 1946-52*; and, of course, at various points in the *Church Dogmatics* (e.g., II/2, 721-23 ff.; III/4, 455-56, among others). For an extensive and helpful analysis of the relationship between Barth's own theology and his view of communism, see West, *Communism and the Theologians*, 177-325.

12. In contrast to the thesis of Friedrich-Wilhelm Marquardt who sees Barth, first and foremost, as a political theologian; see Marquardt, *Theologie und Sozialismus*; see also various reactions to Marquardt's thesis in Hunsinger, *Karl Barth and Radical Politics*.

In the letters and writings while in prison Bonhoeffer began to consider the present and future condition of Protestant Christianity. His thought focused on the place of the church in "a world come of age," a world that no longer needed God to explain heretofore mysterious natural phenomena, a world where religion was not only dispensable but also harmful in terms of perpetuating unnecessary myths about God and God's relationship with the world.

In addition to "a world come of age," we find in Bonhoeffer's letters such language as "religionless Christianity," "a world without God," "God as a stop-gap," "the powerlessness of God in the world," and "the church for others." Because Bonhoeffer died before he was able to develop these ideas further, it is not clear in what direction these thoughts would have taken him. In contrast to some interpreters of Bonhoeffer, Eberhard Bethge, Bonhoeffer's friend, colleague, and biographer, sees a continuity between Bonhoeffer's earlier writings and his prison writings rather than a discontinuity:

> People's surprise led them to get out again the early works of Bonhoeffer that had not received much attention hitherto and to discover with astonishment that there was a broad continuity between the Berlin beginnings and the Tegel period. Formulations and theological hints in *Letters and Papers from Prison* that people found shocking proved not to be as new as had been thought and were to be found, even literally, in *Sanctorum Communio* or *Act and Being*, as well as in other writings.[13]

However, since the publication of *Letters and Papers from Prison*, serious attention has been given to those letters and papers as representing a new trajectory in Bonhoeffer's thought, and some have sought to find in them a description of the relationship between Christianity and society in the modern and post-modern world as well as a prescription for the life of the church in this world. Thomas I. Day has written:

---

13. Bethge, *Dietrich Bonhoeffer*, 792–93.

Dietrich Bonhoeffer's theology has been a Ouija board. As many as have put their hand to it have read different messages, pertinent and crucial but mutually contradictory and generally confusing. As Lenin suggested in another case, the plethora of interpretations and revisions reflect not so much the weakness of Bonhoeffer's work as the fact that his theology impinges on the lives of those who take it up. If geometric axioms affected human interests, attempts would certainly be made to refute them.[14]

From John A. T. Robinson's *Honest to God* to the "death of God" theology in the 1960s to American black theology to various forms of liberation theology found, for example, in South Africa and Latin America,[15] the theological seeds in Bonhoeffer's *Letters and Papers* have taken root and his influence is unquestionable. However, it is impossible to say whether or not Bonhoeffer himself would have endorsed these trends which claim a debt to his thought, including those who deliberately chose to live in a communist society.

Although the attempt at a communist takeover that began in Kiel following World War I was short-lived, communism became a reality for eastern Germany and most of eastern Europe following World War II, and the thought of Barth and Bonhoeffer came to be a powerful influence there as well as in the rest of western Christianity. For the first time since the rise of communism a land that was predominantly Protestant would face the challenge of existing under a communist system.

Clearly, the thought of Karl Barth and Dietrich Bonhoeffer exercised a profound influence on the theology and the church in what became the German Democratic Republic. It is equally clear that Barth's 1919 lecture in Tambach was addressed to and was critical of religious socialists who sought to find some kind of synthesis between socialism and religion (especially Christianity). Given the distance in time since the fall of communism in eastern Germany in 1989, it is appropriate and instructive to examine, on

14. Day, "Essay Review," 117.

15. See Robinson, *Honest to God*; Altizer and Hamilton, *Radical Theology and the Death of God*; Cone, *Black Theology & Black Power*; DeGruchy, *Dietrich Bonhoeffer and South Africa*; Gutierrez, *A Theology of Liberation*.

the one hand, the writings of an East German theologian who both claimed a debt to Barth and Bonhoeffer and at the same time was an ardent supporter of the Communist regime and, on the other hand, the sermons of some pastor-theologians who struggled to find some kind of accommodation within the Communist system without succumbing to it.

Hanfried Müller was born in Celle (near Hanover) in 1925. He was baptized in the Lutheran church, and grew up and was confirmed in the "united" church in the Rhineland. His Reformed tendencies originally derived, at least initially, not so much from confessional convictions as from a relationship he and his wife enjoyed with a Reformed pastor in Berlin, Heinrich Grüber. One source identifies Grüber as "since 1949 the authorized agent [Bevollmächtigter"] of the EKiD [Evangelical Church in Germany] in the government of the GDR."[16] Müller describes his parents as having been "anti-Nazi." As a youngster he came into contact with the Confessing Church through a "student Bible class" ("Schülerbibelkreis"). He served in the German army during World War II in Italy and was, for a brief time, an American prisoner-of-war.[17]

In November 1945, Müller began his theological studies at the University of Bonn. In 1947, he continued his studies at the University of Göttingen under Hans Iwand and Ernst Wolf.

His (unpublished) dissertation on the "Influence of Existentialism on Evangelical Theology Today" ("Einfluß des Existentialismus auf die evangelische Theologie der Gegenwart") was not

---

16. Linke, *Theologiestudenten der Humboldt-Universität*, 16. In *"Pfarrer, Christen und Katholiken,"* Besier and Wolf provide additional biographical information about Grüber. He lived 1891-1975. He studied theology and philosophy in Bonn, Berlin, and Utrecht, participated in World War I as a metal worker, and was ordained in 1920. He served several pastorates during the Weimar and early Hitler years. From 1940 to 1943 he was in concentration camps in Sachsenhausen and Dachau. Among other activities following World War II he was one of the founders of the Evangelische Verlagsanstalt in Berlin. From 1949 to 1958 he was "the authorized agent of the Council of the Evangelical Church in Germany in the government of the GDR ("Bevollmächtigter des Rates der EKD bei der Regierung der DDR"). In 1970 he became an honorary citizen of Berlin (810).

17. Letter from Müller to the author, dated July 19, 1991.

approved due, in his words, to "disciplinary proceedings that were politically motivated."[18] Müller attributes this action to his participation in proscribed demonstrations against military rearmament in western Germany. Because of these charges against him, Müller was arrested and not permitted to take his doctoral exams.[19] In 1952 he and his wife moved to East Berlin (illegally, he acknowledges, because the British authorities denied him permission to move). Both Müller and his wife applied to the state for graduate study and, in 1952, both were assigned ("zugewiesen") to the theological faculty of Humboldt University.[20] Müller completed his doctoral exams there and wrote his dissertation on Dietrich Bonhoeffer (later published as *Von der Kirche zur Welt*). From 1959 to 1964 he was a lecturer at Humboldt. In 1964 he became professor there and was appointed full professor of systematic theology in 1966.[21]

In his volume of collected documents detailing the influence of the Communist authorities on the theological faculty at Humboldt University, Dietmar Linke has written the following regarding Hanfried Müller and his wife, Rosemarie Müller-Streisand:

> The situation of the Müller couple was distinguished from that of other colleagues on the faculty in that, by emigrating, they had demonstrated a conscious decision for theGDR. In their "baggage" they had no negative experiences from the discussions between state and church. Unencumbered, they were able to use their "good" relationship to the state for their own interests. Consistent with their own background, they were interested in recruiting students to work with them in the FDJ [Free GermanYouth]. From the perspective of the state, there was enthusiastic interest in them both, in building and advancing the "most positive forces on the faculty" in order to repress the influence of the "reactionary forces."[22]

18. Letter from Müller to the author, dated July 19, 1991.
19. Linke, *Theologiestudenten der Humboldt-Universität*, 41.
20. Linke, *Theologiestudenten der Humboldt-Universität*, 41.
21. Linke, *Theologiestudenten der Humboldt-Universität*, 44.
22. Linke, *Theologiestudenten der Humboldt-Universität*, 42.

Linke also documents the fact that the promotion of both the Müllers to positions of professor was not greeted with unanimous agreement among members of the theological faculty. Walter Elliger, professor of church history and director of the Institute for Christian Archaeology and Church Art, along with Professor Erich Fascher, opposed the appointment of Hanfried Müller to professor.[23] Elliger, who had been at Humboldt since 1950, and against whom the university had taken disciplinary measures in 1961 because he had stated that "as a Christian, he no longer had any confidence in our state,"[24] was allowed to accept a position in Bochum (West Germany) in 1963.

Apparently, Müller found himself often at odds with members of the Christian Democratic Union (CDU), a political party that sought to represent the church and church-related interests. In this regard, Linke writes:

> It is obvious that the opposition between the Müller-faction and the CDU-faction essentially defined the situation of the Berlin theological faculty/section up to the Wende in 1989. It is equally obvious that in these decades H. Müller repeatedly made use of students in order to advance his interests, to procure information, to stifle other lecturers, and to guide disciplinary proceedings against students.[25]

Linke also notes that, beginning in the mid-1960s, Müller was the theological faculty representative to the Synod of Berlin-Brandenburg, a position that allowed him also to represent the government's positions to the church.[26]

The construction of the Berlin Wall on August 13, 1961 had its impact on the theological faculty at Humboldt University. On October 4 of that year a faculty meeting took place in which Müller and his wife, lecturers at the time, participated. Dietmar Linke

---

23. Linke, *Theologiestudenten der Humboldt-Universität*, 43.
24. Linke, *Theologiestudenten der Humboldt-Universität*, 33.
25. Linke, *Theologiestudenten der Humboldt-Universität*, 45–46.
26. Linke, *Theologiestudenten der Humboldt-Universität*, 44–45.

has published the minutes of that meeting.[27] The record summarizes the comments and exchanges of the participants. According to the scribe, the two central issues under discussion were (a) the strengthening of socialism and (b) service in the army.[28] Müller's contributions to the discussion are revealing. Early on, the conversation revolved around war and peace with the issue of reunification in the background. In response to Prorektor Naumann's observation that peace was more important than reunification and that atomic weapons had been forced on the GDR, Müller concurred: "The battle against rearmament of West Germany is lost. The strengthening of the GDR is the only means of preventing atomic war."[29]

Later in the same meeting, after it was agreed that theological students had a military responsibility (pacifism was unacceptable), the issue of the church arose. The following is the clerk's summary of an exchange involving Müller:

> Vogel: Our task is not to provide a theological agreement to a particular policy.
> Strasser: (inquires about the formulation Naumann had begun)
> Fessen: The issue is not a theological agreement, but rather a political declaration.
> Müller: The question of those refusing military service is not the central question. The central question is the actual internal recognition of the GDR.
> Rose: Müller always talks of the church generally. But what is at stake has nothing to do with general appearances. It is gradually becoming intolerable that Müller always apostrophizes the church.
> Müller: Whatever I say against the church, I always say against myself. But I hate Dibelius, Lilie and their consorts.
> Schneider: Where does Müller cooperate with the church?

27. Linke, *Theologiestudenten der Humboldt-Universität*, 153–61.
28. Linke, *Theologiestudenten der Humboldt-Universität*, 153.
29. Linke, *Theologiestudenten der Humboldt-Universität*, 154.

Müller: The church will not let me! (a vigorous dispute with Schneider in the course of which Müller compared the outsider character of his message to that of a prophet.)[30]

In a remarkable way, this exchange reveals something of Müller's view of his own relationship to the East German church, that is, not accepted by the church and, as such, a view of himself as a prophet. Incidentally, the declaration that was finally adopted by the theological faculty was one that, according to Linke, was based on a draft composed by Müller. It affirms the right of the GDR to defend itself and to work toward peace in Europe. In the penultimate paragraph one finds the following statement:

> The theological faculty deeply regrets that developments since 1945 have not led to the establishment of an undivided, militarily neutral, democratic and peace-loving German republic as a whole. However, their responsibility for this unfortunate development as well as for the present danger of war and the resulting painful effects of our situation rests with all those who, in an uninformed way, refused to recognize German guilt and its consequences, and did not abandon their militaristic and aggressive West German policy, as required by the Potsdam Agreement.[31]

Linke observes that the adoption of this declaration by the theological faculty represented a victory for the "progressive forces," a victory that was in accord with the views of the leadership of the university.[32]

---

30. Linke, *Theologiestudenten der Humboldt-Universität*, 156. Otto Dibelius (1880–1967) was staunchly anti-communist and was bishop of the Evangelical Church in Berlin-Brandenburg, which covered an area that included all of Berlin and parts of East Germany. Hanns Lilje (1899–1977) was involved with the Confessing Church from its beginnings in 1933. After World War II he became the bishop of the Evangelical Lutheran State Church of Hanover (in West Germany). He is considered one of the pioneers of the twentieth-century ecumenical movement.

31. Linke, *Theologiestudenten der Humboldt-Universität*, 159.

32. Linke, *Theologiestudenten der Humboldt-Universität*, 159.

Müller remained at Humboldt University in East Berlin until his retirement in 1990. In retirement he edited, published, and wrote for the left-wing theological journal, *Die Weißenseer Blätter*.[33]

In 1995 Müller maintained that he "never formally studied Marxism," that in this regard he was "self-taught."[34] He goes on to write:

> Having grown up without any contact with Communists or Marxism, during the war while recovering in the hospital in Bethel I came across in the church library there Marx's "Kapital," which apparently had been overlooked in the purging of the library by the Nazis; as something forbidden, it was attractive to me. I was completely surprised by the theoretical depth of the work—I had not thought that Communists could think, but I honestly understood very little of what I read. Then as a Wehrmacht soldier in Italy, I had some practical encounters with some partisans who were certainly, in large part, Communists. In 1945/46 in Bonn I became interested in the emerging political parties, including especially the Communists, as they, along with the German Jews, were for us those to whom we bourgeois opponents of Hitler had failed to offer solidarity. With this perspective, in 1948/9 I participated in Göttingen in a "working group for the study of Marxism" in which under the leadership of the Social Democrat sociologist, Dieter Goldschmidt (later at the "free" University in West Berlin) we read the Communist Manifesto. There there was the FDJ-Hochschulgruppe [Free German Youth-College Group] which we founded in 1949/50 in Göttingen, a Marxist independent study group; later at the Humboldt University in Berlin

---

33. Begun in 1982, this journal is an outgrowth of a group of left-wing theologians known as the Weißenseer Arbeitskreis (WAK) which, although having its roots in the Confessing Church during the Hitler period, was revived and reorganized in 1958. Müller notes that this journal originated in 1982 to bridge the sense of discontinuity that arose from the relatively calm relations between church and state following the March 6 meeting between Honecker and church authorities (led by Schönherr).

34. Letter from Hanfried Müller to the author, dated August 28, 1995.

there was the opportunity to participate in further Marxist studies. What certainly influenced me even more was reading the works of Marx and Engels in connection with a growing awareness of the presence in church history of class struggles in every period. But I have never "studied" Marxism either in fact or even systematically.[35]

Published documents in the East German secret police (Stasi) files also indicate that Müller served as an informant to the Stasi from November 1954 until the fall of the East German regime in 1989.[36] Those files reveal the theological graduate student to be eager and willing to inform on churchmen and university faculty members. Müller's code name with the Stasi was "Hans Meier" (sometimes referred to simply as "M"). The following excerpt is from the initial Stasi report on the recruitment of Müller. It is dated December 13, 1954 and is recorded by a Second Lieutenant Kullik:

> M. has scholarly ambitions in theology at the Humboldt University in Berlin. We became aware of him through the GI [Geheimer Informant, "secret informant"] "Anton," who spoke with Müller and his wife regarding preparations for the church conference ["Kirchentag] in Leipzig. In this conversation Müller and his wife expressed a negative attitude toward all the speakers and other church leaders with the exception of Heinemann and Niemöller. After a thorough explanation and description of the proposal to enlist Müller as a secret informant, he was visited by Gen. Sgraja and Gen. Kullik on 29.10.1954 for the first conference in his home. The introduction took place there as representatives of the MdI [Ministry of the Interior] and then later as representatives of SfS [State Secretary of State Security]. In the discussion we explained to Müller that as an organ of security we would like for him to inform us about the situation of the theological faculty. M. demonstrated a complete understanding of that and began to report to us. In this account he inquired as to whether it might be possible to publish a German theological journal. He

---

35. Letter from Hanfried Müller to the author, dated August 28, 1995.
36. Linke, *Theologiestudenten der Humboldt-Universität*, 450.

was very interested in this and would be happy to work, together with his wife, on it. M. described to us the particular professors on the theological faculty and told us about his studies in Göttingen where he also enjoyed the full support of Prof. Wolf and Prof. Iwand in his work in society ["in gesellschaftlicher Arbeit"]. Prof. Wolf and Prof. Iwand belong to his close circle of friends in West Germany. Because of time constraints, another discussion with M. was scheduled for 3.11.1954 at the MdI.

M. appeared on time for the scheduled meeting at the MdI and was then asked to sign an agreement to work with the MdI. Both in prior conversation with him as well as in the written agreement, he demonstrated a very open attitude. He explained to us that we needed to treat his statements with great confidentiality because otherwise news of certain things among the church leadership could have negative consequences for him. It was explained to him that everything he shared with us would be held in the strictest confidence. M. signed the written agreement without any objection. M. himself suggested the cover name "Hans Meier." On the day of the agreement he delivered to us the entire exchange of letters between him and Niemöller for examination. Brief evaluation: In his conduct Müller is very open, talkative, and forthcoming. His attitude toward democratic development is good. Because of connections to, and knowledge of, ecclesiastical, theological issues, he will be able to report to us concerning many matters, including events in church politics; he will also be able to provide proposals regarding some issues. His wife also has scholarly aspirations and also opposes Adenauer's politics and the views of the leading church people. Besides connections with theologians, M. has connections to CDU functionaries like (...) and (...). Working in cooperation with M., we will, over time, be able to develop a good informant.[37]

When asked, in 1995, to comment upon Müller's connections with the East German authorities, Michael Beintker, a contemporary of

37. Linke, *Theologiestudenten der Humboldt-Universität*, 451-52.

Müller and a professor of theology at the University of Halle (an der Saale), made reference to this collection of Stasi documents and clearly considered them authentic. While in Halle, Beintker, later at the University of Münster, had actively opposed the East German regime and found himself under surveillance by government informants.[38]

In May 1993 in Frankfurt Müller addressed an organization called "Science & Socialism" ("Wissenschaft & Sozialismus"). The title of his address was "Congratulations from an Outsider on the 175th Birthday of Karl Marx: On the Encounter of a Dialectical Theologian with Scientific Socialism."[39] In this presentation Müller recalls the internal conflict and contradiction he felt as a 20-year-old at the end of World War II. On the one hand, he had not subscribed to Nazism; indeed, as a youth he had become active in the Confessing Church. On the other hand, he had participated in the war and, therefore, shared the guilt of war crimes and crimes against humanity. "And out of this question of guilt arose the question of how fascism and war are made and how they can be prevented."[40]

In this 1993 attempt to address this question, Müller maintained that he found answers from the church unsatisfactory. The Confessing Church, while being anti-Nazi and anti-Hitler, had succumbed to "genuinely clerical fascism"—not only in its opposition to the Nazi Party and its support for Franco in the Spanish Civil War, but also in taking the middle "against 'National Socialism and Stalinism' with their call to struggle against all 'totalitarianism.'" This middle position, which opposed both the nationalist extremists on the right and the Communist extremists on the left,

---

38. Beintker's reference to the Stasi documents in the Linke volume appears in a letter to the author, dated November 29, 1995. Beintker's reference to his own experience in the GDR came from a personal conversation between him and the author in his home in Halle in May 1991.

39. Müller, "Gratulation eines Außenseiters zum 175."

40. Müller, "Gratulation eines Außenseiters zum 175." 31.

reflected the church's desire to protect its own interests, according to Müller.[41]

Müller also found no help in answers provided by "bourgeois democrats" ('bürgerliche Demokraten"). After all, National Socialism had arisen "from an order in state and society [. . .] which had almost seemed to be a model democracy and whose 'Weimar constitution' was idolized at the time no less than the 'Basic Law' of the FRG.'"[42] It gave Müller great pause to think that a social democrat friend of his parents felt he had to respect the decision of the people to choose a government under Hitler ("if the majority of the German people indicated in a free election that they desired a government under Hitler, he would have to respect it as such").[43]

Only the Communists were able to answer satisfactorily the question that had plagued Müller and his friends at the end of World War II. Writing in 1993, Müller maintained:

> Thus to my surprise it was the *Communists* who were able to answer our question. They were able not only to explain who, why, and by what means war and fascism were evoked, but they were also able to show that they had warned of this ahead of time: "Whoever votes for Hindenburg, votes for Hitler; whoever votes for Hitler, votes for war." And they had an understanding of democracy which not only permitted but demanded extra-parliamentary opposition to the German-national–National Socialist coalition government which was constituted according to all rules of Parliament—even at the risk of one's own life.[44]

While Müller found clericalism and "bourgeois democrats" lacking in being able to answer his questions satisfactorily, it is interesting that he found answers to his questions in communism and Communist Party ideology and not in his chosen field of academic study, theology. At the very least, this fact raises the question as

---

41. Müller, "Gratulation eines Außenseiters zum 175," 31.
42. Müller, "Gratulation eines Außenseiters zum 175," 31.
43. Müller, "Gratulation eines Außenseiters zum 175," 31.
44. Müller, "Gratulation eines Außenseiters zum 175," 31–32.

to which, for him, came first. His critique of the church and of western democracy may well be valid, but, among other things, it ignores the refusal of the Communists to make common cause with the opponents to Hitler. Clearly, his Marxist leanings influenced his theology more than his theology informed his Marxist tendencies. He identifies himself as an "outsider" to his audience, presumably because he considers himself a theologian first and a Marxist second. And yet, his closing words in this 1993 address in Frankfurt suggest at least an equal commitment to Marxist ideology as to Christian theology:

> I wish for you and us that you will not retract or surrender the historical-dialectical-materialistic consciousness, that you will not capitulate after the defeat but will use the time of counterrevolutionary crisis to re-establish and develop further this consciousness, and that as those who are now defeated you will rise again with the proud statement: "And the revolution continues!"—not only the earth around the sun, but with the punishment of the loss of all civilization and culture also human society to Communism![45]

In 1954 Müller published an essay in the form of a pamphlet that bore the title "The Christian in Church and State" ("Der Christ in Kirche und Staat"). Using the Barmen Declaration as his basis, particularly the fifth thesis,[46] Müller sets forth his understanding of the proper relationship between church and state and the role of the Christian in society. A brief examination of this paper will demonstrate two characteristics of Müller's thought: first, his language reveals a Marxist view of history; and second, his view of church and state is what Robert Goeckel describes as "a radical separation of the worldly and spiritual kingdoms."[47]

---

45. Müller, "Gratulation eines Außenseiters zum 175," 54.

46. The fifth thesis is based on 1 Peter 2:17: "Fear God, honor the king!" See Leith, *Creeds of the Churches*, 521.

47. Goeckel, *The Lutheran Church and the East German State*, 98, footnote 36.

At the outset Müller sets the issue in a twofold manner: (a) the Christian in the state and the political ethics of the Christian and (b) the Christian in the church and the discipleship of the true church.[48] He then defines the nature of each:

> The church is a matter of faith and proclamation. In its essence it is hidden to human science and natural understanding; it is appropriated only in faith where human perception is able to see nothing other than a religious community. On the other hand, the state is a matter of scientific investigation and ideological knowledge; in contrast to the church it is precisely and entity that is evident and not hidden, one that is accessible to knowledge and not faith.[49]

In distinguishing between the two, Müller also makes a point that he will pursue throughout his writings, namely, that the church is only rightly understood when it is in the service of Jesus Christ; this is a point which in itself may be indisputable but which will lead Müller to a somewhat more controversial view of the church:

> This distinction between state and church, however, postulates that one can speak of the state only in objective terms because it speaks scientifically and rationally and therefore in the name of and in obligation to rational understanding, whereas with regard to the church one can only speak appropriately in the name of Jesus Christ himself and thus in testimony to the faith. But neither here nor there may one speak in the name of the church. [. . .][50]

The state, then, can be viewed as a matter that is subject to scientific human reason, while the church can only be discussed in terms of faith that seeks to serve Jesus Christ. In short, the state and its purpose are objective and visible, while the church and its

---

48. Müller, "Der Christ in Kirche und Staat," 6. The original reads: "1. Der Christ im Staat und die politische Ethik des Christen. 2. Der Christ in der Kirche und die Nachfolge der wahren Kirche."

49. Müller, "Der Christ in Kirche und Staat," 6.

50. Müller, "Der Christ in Kirche und Staat," 6.

mission are subjective and hidden, or at least not as readily evident to those outside the church as to those inside the church.

But then Müller, in this 1958 essay, discusses the way in which the view of the state has changed since New Testament times. Of particular significance and interest is the language he uses to do so:

> The first significant change in the view of the state occurred when the bourgeois revolution understood the state in terms of the sovereignty of the people—and thus burdened every person, every Christian also, whether he wished it or not, with civic, and therefore, public responsibility. The second important shift in the view of the state was brought by the proletarian revolution which understood the state as an organized political power of the ruling class over the oppressed class—and therefore revealed the utopian-illusionary character of the bourgeois sovereignty of the people, but at the same time provided an historical perspective to the realization of the principle "All power proceeds from the people"; this also burdened substantively every person with political responsibility for which he takes part in the class struggle. If the view of the state brought by the bourgeois revolution contributed, above all, the formal and individual and only apparent participation of all citizens in political responsibility, then the socialistic view of the state contributed the substantive and collective and real involvement of the masses in the political responsibility vis-a-vis the state or for the state.[51]

Müller's understanding of the history of the development of the state is couched in terms of "bourgeois," "class struggle," "proletariat," "masses," "oppressed class," and "socialism."

Furthermore, he argues that not only has class struggle been a perennial problem of the state, but it has been one for the church as well. Müller sees an opportunity for this problem to be addressed, if not altogether resolved, in a modern socialist state:

> All of church history shows us how in the church's class ties the gospel became repeatedly untrustworthy

---

51. Müller, "Der Christ in Kirche und Staat," 7–8.

[unglaubwürdig]. But what is new, in fact, is the awareness of this problem in light of the class struggle. The resolution of this problem might be a crucial task of dogmatics and ethics in our generation.[52]

Noting that both church and state are part of "the yet unredeemed world" (language of Thesis 5 in the Barmen Declaration),[53] Müller argues that

> [t]he church of forgiven sinners stands in complete solidarity with this world in as much as God's grace is meant for this world and it is meant for the church in so far as the church belongs to this world. [. . .] In the church's relationship with the state, with which it exists together in the still unredeemed world, the church can never claim a greater righteousness or dignity.[54]

The task of the just state is to work for justice and peace. It may employ force only in the service of that objective. Interestingly, Müller does not define what he means by justice and peace. But the church, because it is part of the still unredeemed world along with the state, has no right to interfere with the state's responsibility to preserve justice and peace. However, the Christian does have a responsibility not only to support the state in its responsibility, but also to be engaged politically:

> Along with the criterion of the just state in its concern for justice and peace there is also the criterion of the Christian's political role in the class struggle. [. . .] It is impossible to demand neutrality in the class struggle from the Christian who acts responsibly in political matters because every political or indirectly political activity is participation in the class struggle. The church,

---

52. Müller, "Der Christ in Kirche und Staat," 9.

53. The first paragraph of Thesis 5 reads: "The Bible tells us that according to divine arrangement the state has the responsibility to provide for justice and peace in the yet unredeemed world, in which the church also stands, according to the measure of human insight and human possibility, by the threat and use of force" (Leith, *Creeds*, 521).

54. Müller, "Der Christ in Kirche und Staat," 12.

however, must be neutralized in the class struggle for the sake of the freedom of the Word of God.[55]

So, Christians must be politically engaged in the class struggle because they belong to the same unredeemed world as non-Christians, but the church, for the sake of the freedom of the Word of God, must be neutral (or "be neutralized"). This takes place, Müller explains,

> in that in Barmen the political role is tied to the understanding and ability of the individual in obedience to the gospel, but not directly to the gospel itself which would then, in fact, become law. It is a narrow path that is walked—the limits described here cannot be explicated in detail here.[56]

The distinction Müller seems to be making is that the Christian, out of obedience to the gospel, has a political responsibility to the state, society, and the world, but that that responsibility is not to try to make the world conform to the gospel. Or, to put it another way, the church is not to dominate or clericalize the state, society, or the world.

What, then, is the task of the church? Müller writes:

> If the criterion for a just state is the concern for justice and peace, the true church finds its criterion in the freedom of God's grace: "With her faith as well as her obedience, with her message as well as her ordinances, she has to witness in the midst of the world of sin as the church of forgiven sinners..." (Barmen 3). "The commission of the church," according to Barmen 6, "in which her freedom is founded, consists in this: in place of Christ and thus in the service of his own word and work, to extend through word and sacrament the message of the free grace of God to all people." Wherever it departs from this charge or goes beyond it, it ceases to be the true church.[57]

---

55. Müller, "Der Christ in Kirche und Staat," 15–16.
56. Müller, "Der Christ in Kirche und Staat," 16.
57. Müller, "Der Christ in Kirche und Staat," 19.

Consequently, the church "may neither clericalize the state nor secularize itself."[58] Although Müller fails to define what justice and peace mean in terms of the responsibility of the state, he finds Barmen's definition of the responsibility of the church satisfactory, namely, "to witness in the midst of the world of sin as the church of forgiven sinners."[59]

Interestingly, Müller makes only passing reference to the conclusion of Thesis 5, namely, "We repudiate the false teaching that the church can turn over the form of her message and ordinances at will or according to some dominant ideological and political convictions."[60] Although this may have originally referred to Nazi ideology, and although Müller concedes that Barmen does not require a socialist perspective,[61] by his own commitment to Marxism Müller has not only misunderstood and misinterpreted Barth and Bonhoeffer, but he has also allowed that commitment to dominate his theology.

Finally, Müller's program inevitably causes him to succumb, no doubt unwittingly, to the temptation to synthesize socialist ideology and Christian theology, something Barth condemned in his address at Tambach in 1919. Thus, when for the first time Christianity could be tested in a Communist-dominated state, Müller's perspective reflects the failure of this synthesis. While he would, no doubt, reject this interpretation of his work, it seems that his writings, at the very least, leave themselves open to this interpretation, and, at the most, confirm it.

There were theologians in the former German Democratic Republic who were equally influenced by the thought of the Barth and Bonhoeffer, and who struggled mightily with what it meant to be the church in a socialist and totalitarian state. However, they did not share Müller's commitment to Marxist ideology. Indeed,

---

58. Müller, "Der Christ in Kirche und Staat," 19. The original reads: "Die Kirche hat weder die Möglichkeit, den Staat zu klerikalisieren, noch sich selbst to säkularisieren."
59. Leith, *Creeds*, 521.
60. Leith, *Creeds*, 521.
61. Müller, "Der Christ in Kirche und Staat," 17.

that was part of their struggle—how to be the church under an ideology with which they disagreed or which, at the very least, limited their ability to be the church. Even if some may have sympathized with Marxist socialism, that does not necessarily mean subjugating their theological and faith convictions to that particular ideology. Müller found himself more at odds with the church than with the East German Marxist state and its ideology. We will now examine how this ideology is reflected in the language of his writings.

CHAPTER 4

Müller's Language and Ideology

IN THE MAY 1991 issue of *Kirchliche Zeitgeschichte* Michael Beintker, professor of theology at the University of Halle (an der Saale) and an activist in opposition to the government of the former German Democratic Republic, published an article under the title "Die Idee des Friedens als Waffe im Kalten Krieg" ("The Idea of Peace as a Weapon in the Cold War").[1] In this article Beintker takes to task those theologians and churchmen in the former GDR who in their perspectives superimposed their Marxist-Leninist ideology on their theology. Specifically, he notes the way in which the biblical notion of peace is transformed to suit their purposes and how those who disagreed with their perspective must have been against peace, socialism, and the GDR. He writes:

> The infamy of the process of accumulating all peace-loving powers for "our cause" consisted in the clumsy, but effective elimination of critical consciousness, the expressed renunciation of a free way of thinking of the ideological model of the East-West conflict, and in the imposition of guilty consciences: If socialism = peace,

---

1. Beintker, "Die Idee des Friedens als Waffe im Kalten Krieg."

and if the GDR = socialism, then you must be ashamed of yourself if as a Christian you are critical of the GDR, for you are then against peace (and, in effect, for imperialistic politics of aggression).[2]

Beintker goes on to observe that those who adopted such a perspective

> saw themselves as being on the only correct theological course; they made reference to that which [. . .] was a most cunning political domestication of theology, namely, to the Barmen Declaration, to Karl Barth and Dietrich Bonhoeffer, Martin Niemöller and Hans-Joachim Iwand; as the majority they saw themselves as the rightful heirs to the Confessing Church and charged with carrying out the legacy "obstructed by the EKD."[3]

He refers to this approach as "pseudo-theology" and includes Hanfried Müller (and Müller's wife, Rosemarie Müller-Streisand, a church historian) among those who engaged in it. Noting how the Barmen Declaration was used to justify support for the SED[4] government in the GDR, Beintker writes:

> In effect, the position in the "anti-imperialistic struggle" became a *current* confessional question, grounded in orthodox terms and following the party line. "The great question in theology," wrote Hanfried Müller in 1974, "appears to me today—as it has always been—to be the question: Do we rely on our Christian self-understanding, world relations, or theologies which in their appended genitive reveal the gods whom they serve in addition to Christ." Such theological clarity, which Hanfried Müller also intended for the adamant opponents of

---

2. Beintker, "Die Idee des Friedens als Waffe im Kalten Krieg," 255.

3. Beintker, "Die Idee des Friedens als Waffe im Kalten Krieg," 256. Iwand (1899–1960) was a Lutheran theologian who was greatly influenced by Karl Barth and who taught first at the University of Göttingen and later at the University of Bonn.

4. Sozialistische Einheitspartei Deutschland (Socialist Unity Party of Germany), the official Communist Party of the GDR which governed the GDR.

the East-CDU, had to be unveiled in the same context as theological docetism, as a purposeful explanation of the incompetence of theology in the service of peace when Müller then continued, not without reference to the "need to learn" ["Lernbedarf"] in the churches in the DDR: "And the great political question is the class question, the question of socialism, peace, and progress or imperialism, war, and barbarism."[5]

Beintker does not object to critiques of imperialism by theologians such as Müller or by anyone else. Rather, his objection is twofold: first, the adoption by Müller (and others) of critical language that has become full of clichés, and second, the absence of any critical objective analysis of the party line they defend:

> Theologically, defeat of imperialistic powers, especially those which threaten peace, cannot be objected to. Imperialistic powers are always dangerous. But those also played with fire who attacked the "bourgeois" societies of the West with a nebulous cliche of imperialism and at the same time were unable to cultivate the slightest trace of criticism for the imperialism of the socialism, Moscow style, which understood itself as being constantly on the march, as if one were always living in the kingdom of "eternal peace", the perfected democracy where human rights were fully realized.[6]

Beintker's observations are particularly pertinent to the contention of this book. As we have seen in Müller's appropriation of the life and work of Bonhoeffer and Barth, and will see in the writings of Johannes Hamel, it will become increasingly clear that Müller's views are predicated on a particular political-ideological perspective.

In considering Müller's theology, it is essential that we see in concrete terms how Marxist language is reflected in his theological perspective, thus lending credence to Beintker's analysis. In 1977 Müller wrote an introduction to theology under the title

---

5. Beintker, "Die Idee des Friedens als Waffe im Kalten Krieg," 256-7.
6. Beintker, "Die Idee des Friedens als Waffe im Kalten Krieg," 257.

Evangelische Dogmatik im Überblick (*An Introduction to Protestant Dogmatic Theology*).[7] In the Foreword, Müller notes that he had the impression that some persons hoped, while others feared, that his would be a "more political Dogmatics." He continues:

> In the meantime I can imagine that there are also some readers for whom this outline might sound too "political" in many ways. A few observations are in order as to how, in my opinion, Protestant dogmatics must adhere to the right path of theological and political responsibility vis-a-vis a false politicization of theology and vis-a-vis a false apolitical Christianity. Of course dogmatics—even in outline—can be carried out only in an environment which corresponds to the liveliness of Protestant theology and is therefore certainly based on the existence of the theologian which is concretely defined in the here and now and, therefore, is also political. At the same time, the political existence of Christians is constantly the this-worldly, the "non-religious" interpretation of their theological existence today. But this political component can be enjoined directly or indirectly, and it would wrong—especially political—to make the political the main theme.[8]

Claiming that one's political existence may inevitably be part of one's theological reflection, but that one's politics should not be mistaken for theology, Müller so mixes the language of both that it is difficult, if not impossible, to distinguish the two.

In this same Foreword he writes that he does not want to write a political theology or a socialistic theology, but rather

> precisely in view of the ecumenical discussion to conduct good, true Protestant theology in the GDR, in political cooperation with non-Christians, in everyday respect to the tasks, achievements, and problems of socialistic

---

7. Müller, *Evangelische Dogmatik im Überblick*.

8. Müller, *Evangelische Dogmatik im Überblick*, 15–16. The term "non-religious" is one of several terms coined by Dietrich Bonhoeffer in his letters from prison. See Bonhoeffer, *Letters and Papers from Prison*, 300, 344, 362.

society. I consider this to be precisely a–by the way, the only Christian specific—politicum.⁹

Even if Müller's intent is to write a theology which contributes to the ecumenical discussion by addressing life in the GDR, one must ask the extent to which he can do this fairly without a critical eye toward the very society in which he lives. In other words, while he may deal with the "tasks, achievements, and problems of socialistic society," can he do so without at least calling into question the presuppositions of that society?

Müller's attribution to his anticipated critics of "imperialism" of one form or another betrays his own (political) ideological commitment, thus rendering his theological assertions, whatever they may be, suspect—at least in terms of their theological integrity, independent of any ideological or political convictions. In reading what Müller writes, for example, one soon discovers that "imperialism" is almost always a reference to western capitalism. Furthermore, theology as practiced in the western world as a rule inevitably reflects an unconscious adherence to, and implicit support of, capitalism and all the sins that accompany it (anti-socialism, anti-Bolshevism, civil religion, exploitation of the poor for economic gain, among others). Thus, Michael Beintker's observation begins to ring true, namely, that Müller reflects the East-West mentality which finds everything wrong on the other side, but refuses to exercise the same kind of critical judgment toward one's own political ideology or system.

How, then, are these ideological tendencies and convictions reflected in Müller's own writings? In the following samples we will be able to see the prominence of Müller's political ideology in his thought, both by means of his language as well as in the substance of that language.

Müller's *Evangelische Dogmatik im Überblick* is structured in the form of a catechism. At various points Müller cites Marx and Engels approvingly. In the section "The Existence of God" we find Question 38: "What does the question of God's existence mean in

---

9. Müller, *Evangelische Dogmatik im Überblick*, 16. I understand "politicum" to mean "politics".

terms of one's view of the world?" In the fourth paragraph of his answer, Müller writes:

> [Karl Marx] does not criticize religion as an intellectual-individual error of believers or a deception by priests, but rather he demands the revolutionary change of its underlying conditions. Thus, in this respect he deals with the question of God's existence by understanding and overcoming it in historical terms. "To abolish religion as the illusory happiness of the people is to demand their real happiness. The demand to give up illusions about the existing state of affairs is the demand to give up a state of affairs which needs illusions. The criticism of religion is therefore in embryo the criticismof the vale of tears, the halo of which is religion."[10]

Müller continues this line of thought in a subsequent excursus on "religion and religionlessness." His own Marxist perspective becomes increasingly evident in his references to Ludwig Feuerbach and Marx. Müller writes:

> On the basis of the historically contradictory role of the bourgeoisie there developed in the bourgeois Enlightenment not only plebeian-revolutionary-democratic forms of critiques of religion, as, for example, they found their crowning conclusion in Ludwig Feuerbach, but also aristocratic forms which corresponded to the enlightened absolutism and served to distinguish themselves from all religious demands in order to be able to manipulate religion all the more as an instrument of suppression. Atheism is not indifferent to class. Besides a plebeian atheism, there is also an aristocratic atheism against which Robespierre's protest, with some justification, was aimed: "There are persons who make atheism a kind of religion under the pretext of destroying superstition. But atheism is the business of the aristocracy: the idea of a supreme being that watches over the oppressed innocence and

---

10. Müller, *Evangelische Dogmatik im Überblick*, 67. The quotation is from Marx's *Zur Kritik der Hegelschen Rechtsphilosophie. Einleitung.* The English translation is taken from Marx and Engels, *Collected Works Volume 3*, 176 (the emphasis is in the original).

punishes the triumphant crimes for the people. If God did not exist, one would have to invent him."[11]

In an article appearing in the *Weißenseer Blätter* in 1982,[12] Müller takes up the issue of "dissidents" in communist countries to address the relationship between the church and culture. It will be recalled that it was at this time that the peace movement was beginning to take hold in East Germany, and that many, both in the church and outside the church, were protesting the increase of Soviet missiles in eastern Europe aimed at the West.

The "dissidents" to whom Müller refers are those who rejected socialist and communist ideology and sought refuge in the church. But, as will be seen, Müller's analysis is itself driven by an ideological streak which defends socialist societies and condemns capitalistic, imperialistic ones. At the outset Müller's language makes clear his contempt for those who desert the socialist cause:

> There have always been renegades in socialism. They openly deserted to the bourgeois camp. There they were used for purposes of propaganda—and then forgotten. There have always been deviations from the party line. In the course of history they were dialectically dissolved and, viewed as a whole, served objectively the politically and theoretical maturation of socialistic ideology in the process of differing opinions within the party. But renegades and those with varying opinions rarely came to church. And the bourgeois church saw in them—not without malicious joy that the revolution devours its own children—Communists who remained suspect, even if they were disappointed in, devastated, and failed by their party. The progressive past of such deserters was

---

11. Müller, *Evangelische Dogmatik im Überblick*, 250–1. Müller's quotation in this passage is from Tschackert, "Art. Revolution, französische." Feuerbach was a nineteenth-century philosopher who maintained that Christianity was an illusion. In 1854 he published *Wesen des Christentums* (*The Essence of Christianity*). His influence extended to Friedrich Nietzsche, Richard Wagner, and Karl Marx, among others.

12. Müller, "Randbemerkungen zu einigen Randerscheinungen zwischen Kirche und Kultur."

understandable as a sin of youth which one could jointly forget with them.[13]

Having said that, however, Müller goes on to observe that the "dissidents" were more than "renegades" and "those with varying opinions" within the party. Müller defines "dissidents" as

> those who enjoy the support of anti-Communists and serve them by naming Communists and attacking true socialism by attacking them as comrades of their party. Some of these dissidents have not only run away from their party, but they have run to the church—or have been captured by it. Furthermore, their perspective on life finds an echo at the edges of some of our young congregations.[14]

Thus, Müller finds fault both with "dissidents" and with the church which provides them refuge.

Müller argues that the critique of socialism offered by dissidents "shoots up like weeds in a field and claims an authority which is not warranted." He sees it as

> a sign of the human strength of our socialist society that many of those wanting out, who at one time became Robin Hoods in the decaying feudalism and who would have become terrorists under capitalism's law of the wolf, seize only the pen among us and do not, for the sake of notoriety, resort to bombs and blackmail of their party and state by hostage-taking.[15]

Müller's language not only reflects his commitment to socialism and his contempt for capitalist society, but it also once again reveals his unwillingness or inability to see any critique of socialist society as being valid or legitimate. Was it, for example, only because the socialist society of the GDR was of a higher human order

---

13. Müller, "Randbemerkungen zu einigen Randerscheinungen zwischen Kirche und Kultur," 37.

14. Müller, "Randbemerkungen zu einigen Randerscheinungen zwischen Kirche und Kultur," 37.

15. Müller, "Randbemerkungen zu einigen Randerscheinungen zwischen Kirche und Kultur," 38.

that dissidents resorted only to a pen and not to bombs and other acts of terrorism? Might not the power of the GDR state have had something to do with the hesitation some dissidents might have harbored? And if the socialist state was of such a high and noble character, why did the dissidents want to leave? These questions do not come into the purview of Müller's analysis. Furthermore, this line of argument reveals Müller's starting point, namely, that of a political ideology and not one of theology or of faith.

Later in the same 1982 essay Müller describes the virtues of communism as it is practiced in Marxist societies:

> To be sure, the structure of Communism is also built in order to provide every member of society the social possibility of becoming, according to his personal abilities, a Marx or an Engels; this, however, is impossible under the conditions of capitalism and the period of transition . . . Only under socialism do the conditions exist under which the socialist consciousness can be developed independently and in a disciplined way as an objective programmatic way of thinking for everyone.[16]

In the conclusion of this essay Müller argues that, while bourgeois society has achieved certain successes in science and technology, it has been at the expense of the workers' dependence on the means of production. This increasingly materialistic society has led to a world-view that is equally materialistic and behind which indeed a religious self-understanding has arisen. The result is the gradual death of objective religion (presumably, true Christianity) "with its absolute claim to truth in dogma and ethics" and the rise of a subjective religion (presumably, pseudo-Christianity) which has led to "a supposedly Christian theology which reveals itself to be illusion and, at times, religious demagogy."[17]

He concludes his essay of 1982 with three reasons the socialist society of the GDR is preferable to the capitalist West:

---

16. Müller, "Randbemerkungen zu einigen Randerscheinungen zwischen Kirche und Kultur," 44.

17. Müller, "Randbemerkungen zu einigen Randerscheinungen zwischen Kirche und Kultur," 45.

> First, we also live in and with our socialist society in a world and a time that is fundamentally characterized by the transition from imperialism to socialism. At the same time, however, the basic contradiction of capitalism and the anarchy of its production still governs world economic relations as a whole, and the imperialistic attempts at expansion influence, directly and indirectly, international relations. [...] Here the exploitation of persons by persons persists, here the class struggle rages on, here the imperialistic war still is a threat. [...] Second, imperialism is engaged even today in a merciless campaign of destruction with its pressure for armaments and economic war against the socialist camp in order to escape, in an expansive way, its own crisis situation. This complicates the effectiveness of a socialist planned economy and the uninhibited self-image of the socialist democracy in its collective responsibility for all citizens. Third, our own ideas which govern us do not go unattacked. From beyond our borders the ideas of the ruling class resound in charming variety through our ether, artfully packaged and virtuously shaped, a propaganda which [...] truly reflects the art of calm and peace. [...] Socialism has become too strong to be attacked from the outside only in a flagrant anti-Communism.[18]

Müller not only addresses what he sees as the misguided notions of "dissidents" in socialist societies, but goes on the offensive in attacking the vices of imperialism and capitalism of the West and in defending the virtues of Marxist socialism in which he chose to live.

In 1984 Müller wrote an article for *Standpunkt*, a Protestant monthly periodical that was published in the GDR from 1973 through 1988. The article was entitled "Der Kirchenkampf–Reformation im 20. Jahrhundert" ("The Church Struggle–Reformation in the 20th Century").[19] In this essay Müller compares and contrasts the Reformation of the sixteenth century with the "church

---

18. Müller, "Randbemerkungen zu einigen Randerscheinungen zwischen Kirche und Kultur," 46–47.

19. Müller, "Der Kirchenkampf—Reformation im 20. Jahrhundert."

struggle" of the twentieth century. Traditionally, he argues, "'reformation" in the church has been an attempt to reform the church from within. He writes:

> [A reformation] attacks a church which by means of its entire social existence does not bear witness to the gospel, but rather denies it: a church that "seeks its own", from the most sublime longing for its own salvation to the strenuous desire to rule the world as God's representative on earth. It encounters a church that does not reflect its commission to live for others, but rather seeks to secure its own existence and win a place for itself as it interprets and satisfies social needs in a religious way in order to achieve a social basis and function. Therefore, it opposes a church that (in the same act) falsely adapts itself to society and falsely confronts that society, just as selfish as the world, a kind of secularized church that would like to clericalize the world.

Müller then goes on to observe:

> And this secularization of the church and clericalization of society takes many forms historically: from caesaropapism of the Roman imperial church to the corpus christianum of western feudalism and the "Christian state" of early bourgeois absolutism to the bourgeois "Christian world" that is sublimated in Christian-humanistic education.[20]

In contrast to the sixteenth-century church, Müller writes:

> the bourgeois church certainly played the role of a "moral-religious" support of the capitalistic society, but more as a lackey than as a leader. Correspondingly, the Protestant attack on it did not have the effect of an incendiary spark, but rather of a symptom of the beginning socialist revolution. Therefore, from a social perspective this reformation has a much narrower significance, but from a purely church historical perspective its significance is much broader.[21]

20. Müller, "Der Kirchenkampf—Reformation im 20. Jahrhundert," 20.
21. Müller, "Der Kirchenkampf—Reformation im 20. Jahrhundert," 20–21.

It soon becomes clear that Müller's view of the church and of church history are colored by a Marxist interpretation of history and society. Not only is capitalism seen as evil, but the church in a capitalist society inevitably succumbs to the values and drives of that society, thus becoming its "lackey," according to Müller. Even the church's missionary efforts are a reflection of capitalism's imperialistic tendencies. Thus, historically, the choices before the church have been either to become worldly, like the society in which it exists, or to try to exercise its influence on the worldly powers and thus "clericalize" the world. Hence, for Müller, a third alternative is required and he finds it in a Marxist view of society and the world, a view which, at least in theory, is concerned with the exploited, rejected, dispossessed of the world. In this view the church shares the same concern as the (Marxist) state, and neither sees itself nor is seen by the state as a rival for the power. The church sees itself as sharing the same concern as the state for the powerless, but expresses this concern in the name of Jesus Christ.

After examining and comparing the social and theological crises in 1525–1526 and 1917 in which the response, first by Luther and later by the German Protestant church, was to retreat to a national and social conservatism, Müller goes on to look at the German church in the years of national socialism. His critical analysis once again reveals a prior political influence. He writes:

> This Protestant clericalism, as Otto Dibelius especially viewed it, was based on the social consequences that had been demonstrated in Luther's ties to the princes and his separation from patricians, plebeians, and revolutionary peasants, his pilgrimage from reformation to restoration. The Protestant churches were confined socially to the "other classes" of the Middle Ages. Their class character was typified by a close association with the nobility. They found support among the masses in the peasant class and in those petit bourgeois circles that lived by production and trade of simple wares. But they were precisely the important reserves in the class struggle. The ruling class used them not only as cattle in warfare, but also as an unthinking electoral herd in peacetime. The church

was able to manipulate them in the interest of the ruling class and was honored for doing so. On this rested the new political clericalism. Dibelius expressed this quite openly: "Unhindered, the church was able to develop its extraordinary gift of ruling the masses."[22]

Müller's critique of "Protestant clericalism" may, in fact, be a legitimate one. However, he betrays any pretense to objectivity by arguing with language that reflects his own political bias, namely, "petit bourgeois," "class struggle," and "ruling class."[23] Even if his critique is considered to be legitimate, it loses much of its force due to the subtle suggestion of an ideological agenda. Moreover, one is forced to ask how critical Müller is, or can be, toward his own ideological agenda. In short, how honest is Müller in evaluating his own perspective as well as that which he critiques? This is precisely the question Michael Beintker raises. Müller's objections to Christian nationalism and Christian clericalism are based not so much on theological honesty as on a Marxist interpretation of history and of the contemporary world.

Finally, in 1989, the year of the GDR's downfall, Müller published a remarkable essay in the *Weißenseer Blätter* entitled "Open Letter to My Friends in the SED"[24] in which he offers his critique, as an outsider, of the faulty Communist leadership that led to the

---

22. Müller, "Der Kirchenkampf—Reformation im 20. Jahrhundert," 24. Otto Dibelius (1880-1967) was a Lutheran pastor and cousin to the New Testament scholar Martin Dibelius. Otto Dibelius supported the Confessing Church in the 1930s. In 1945, he became bishop of Berlin and remained in that position until 1966. In 1949, he became the presiding bishop of the Protestant Church in Germany (EKD). In 1954, he became president of the World Council of Churches. He is the object of much of Müller's scorn and wrath because of his staunch opposition to communism in postwar Germany. In 1945, Dibelius helped establish the CDU (Christian Democratic Union), the conservative political party in West Germany. For Müller, Dibelius embodied the church as a selfish institution which not only has self-perpetuation as a principal aim but which also has become one of the pillars that supports capitalist imperialism.

23. In German, "kleinbürgerlich," "Klassenkampf," and "herrschende Klasse," respectively.

24. SED was the Communist Party in East Germany–Sozialistische Einheitspartei Deutschlands (Socialist Unity Party of Germany).

demise of the GDR. As will be seen, this is not a critique of socialism or communism, but of the leadership within the Communist Party of East Germany which, Müller claims, betrayed the ideals and aims of that party. Müller's claim of being an "outsider" is threefold: as a Christian, as a churchman who has had to live with much anti-communism within the church, and as a member of no political party. Thus, Müller ostensibly seeks to maintain some distance between himself and those whom he addresses, namely, former Communist leaders and functionaries in the GDR. And yet, in this role as an "outsider" Müller clearly reveals a prior commitment to Marxist socialism. It is as if Müller's understanding of Christianity can *only* be rightly practiced in a Marxist socialist society.

In this "open letter" Müller addresses three issues: (a) the attack on the GDR by enemies of socialism; (b) the question of followers, renegades, and deserters "in view of your party and the cause of socialism;" and (c) the "question of trust" which "is now raised among you, against you, and throughout the whole of society in the GDR."[25]

Under the first issue Müller considers the condition of the current struggle between imperialism and the Communist movement. He writes:

> In its anti-Communist struggle imperialism has achieved a success. The socialist camp and the international workers movement in most of the imperialist countries have suffered defeats. The revolutionary world movement as a whole is seriously affected by this. I at least am not yet able to ascertain the scale of these losses; but it is also not yet clear . . . how we all will react to these losses. In any case, in light of them we may neither close our eyes nor be resigned to them if we do not want definitively to lose the struggle against imperialism, fascism, and war . . . The engine of contradictions of class and competition in imperialism will not stand still; it continues to move toward a revolutionary world process, but it can also lead to incalculable catastrophes of imperialistic wars, devastation

---

25. Müller, "Offener Brief an Meine Freunde in der SED," 30.

of the earth, and despair in deadly poverty. Many persons who have nothing to do with socialism correctly see that the consolidation of socialism fulfills a function of security for the whole world—whoever does not wish to listen to Communists and their friends would like at least to test carefully such arguments.[26]

Müller's defense of the GDR as a Marxist-Leninist socialist society has more political ideological roots, it seems, than theological ones. The difficulty with this, of course, is that, despite his claim to the contrary, he writes not as an outsider, but as one who quite clearly is inside the Marxist-Leninist circle, and that inevitably colors his theology. This insider status is confirmed when one recalls his willingness and even his desire to serve the Communist government as a secret informant on his colleagues, and to represent the government's policies and wishes with the church structure.

Regarding the second issue of those within the Communist Party who have surreptitiously undermined the cause of socialism or abandoned it altogether, Müller reveals either remarkable naivete or disingenuous self-righteousness when he writes:

> Apparently—and here I must confess that this surprises and disappoints me—among you there are some who had lost the feeling that one should not serve oneself with privileges. I find it particularly painful that among them are also some who because of their courage in the anti-fascist struggle acquired an authority which was their due.

Noting then his own admiration, as a young man, for the ideals of the GDR in its early years, particularly its ostensible tolerance and acceptance of the weak, the poor, the disenfranchised, those rejected by the West, Müller expresses his sense of betrayal with a biblical parallel:

> But then some of your leading comrades behaved like Ananias and Sapphira in Acts (5:1ff.) who gave the appearance of sharing all their wealth with the community, but then secretly withheld some for themselves. I

26. Müller, "Offener Brief an Meine Freunde in der SED," 30.

honestly do not wish for these comrades the same end that came to Ananias and Sapphira, but I would hope for shame and remorse—not because they wanted to allow themselves a comfortable retirement (which they had surely earned!), but rather because they acted secretly.[27]

Throughout his writings Müller points to the evils and temptations of power, wealth, and materialism, especially as they are evident in capitalist societies in the West. And yet, somehow he is unable to imagine political leaders who are committed to Marxist socialism succumbing to the same temptations and evils. Again, either he naively believes so strongly in the purity and rightness of socialism that no one would be tempted to betray it, or he presumes, disingenuously, that his faith in socialism is more authentic than even that of its leaders. In either case, Müller's critique of the Party leadership is not theological, but politically ideological.

Müller concludes this 1989 article with remarks on his third issue, that of trust. The closing paragraph reflects as clearly as elsewhere his ideological priorities:

> I will trust you if in good as well as in difficult days you remain true to your cause: solidarity with the "condemned of this earth", solidarity with the "third" in the "two-thirds societies", solidarity with the poor in the backyards of the imperialistic economic system in the "third world", solidarity (not with those unwilling to achieve but) with those who are incapable of achieving especially in the future in our country and with the rationality of your historical-dialectical analysis of society which must be restored again from ideology of legitimation to a theory which establishes tasks and guides activity; and if, in all of this, you are prepared to stand or fall with the socialistic character of the GDR! The Paris Commune was conquered, but it did not recant. It thereby encouraged the revolutionary process which continues. Guard your dignity! What we need (if we are able in the leadership of the GDR, otherwise in the opposition)

---

27. Müller, "Offener Brief an Meine Freunde in der SED," 33.

is an anti-imperialistic united front in all of Europe. Will you join me, comrades?[28]

The sample of writings provided here not only offers insights into Müller's views, but also the language he employs reveals the priority of his commitment to Marxist socialism over theology and ministry. His theological perspective can only be seen and properly understood from the vantage point of his ideological convictions.

---

28. Müller, "Offener Brief an Meine Freunde in der SED," 38.

CHAPTER 5

The Ministry and Theology of Johannes Hamel

IN HIS INTRODUCTION TO a collection of essays, addresses, and sermons by Johannes Hamel, Charles West reminds the reader that the land between the Elbe and the Oder Rivers that formed the former German Democratic Republic was the homeland of Luther, Bach, and Goethe. Rich in history and in culture, this land was also populated primarily by Protestants—Lutherans, Reformed, and United churches, whereas other countries behind the Iron Curtain were made up mostly of Roman Catholics or Orthodox Christians.

Johannes Hamel was born on November 19, 1911 in Schöningen, a town about 125 miles due west of Berlin. Raised in Berlin and Erfurt, he was the son of a high school principal. From 1930 to 1935 he studied theology in Tübingen, Königsberg, and Halle. He was influenced by the writings of Karl Barth and the New Testament scholar, Julius Schniewind. In 1933, he joined the Nazi stormtroopers, but 18 months later he broke with the Nazi movement, primarily because of the influence of the Confessing Church. Hamel worked with and for the Confessing Church as the traveling secretary of the German Student Christian Movement.[1]

---

1. Hamel, *A Christian in East Germany*, 13–14.

In 1938 he was ordained by the Confessing Church. Because he assisted Jewish members of his community, the Gestapo assigned him to 14 months of factory work. In 1942 he became a soldier, was wounded in the Soviet Union, and eventually became a prisoner of war in Italy.[2]

After the war, Hamel served as pastor to the University of Halle. From 1955 to 1976 he served as lecturer in practical theology at the University of Naumburg. In February 1953 he, along with 70 other churchmen, was arrested and imprisoned in the Halle prison known as "the Red Ox" by the Stasi for his work with church youth. He remained in prison for five months when, following the June 17 uprising, international pressure was brought to bear for his release and the release of the others who had been imprisoned. Hamel retired in 1976. On August 1, 2002, at the age of 90 years, he died in Wernigerode, located on the northern slope of the Harz mountains in the former German Democratic Republic.

In his "Introductory Essay" to the little book *How to Serve God in a Marxist Land*, Robert McAfee Brown writes the following about Hamel's approach to theology and ministry:

> Perhaps the most important thing to see at work here is Hamel's genuine wrestling with a contemporary problem in the light of biblical faith. He does not just pluck a verse from here and there, but tries to examine his own situation in the light of the *full* sweep of the history of the people of God. His starting point is not Marxist ideology. It is not Western democratic ideology. His starting point is the Bible.[3]

Brown's observation not only describes the profound difference between Hanfried Müller's approach to theology and Hamel's, but

---

2. "Johannes Hamel" in the German version of Wikipedia.

3. Barth and Hamel, *How to Serve God in a Marxist Land*, 20. This volume contains a letter from Karl Barth to an East German pastor in which Barth responds to the pastor's questions and concerns about serving God in a communist country. The volume concludes with a letter from Hamel to Barth expressing appreciation for Barth's letter.

it also provides the foundation for Hamel's understanding of how one engages in ministry anywhere.

In September 1953, Hamel gave an address to an ecumenical conference on Bible study at Bossey, Switzerland. The address was entitled "Preaching and the Bible." He opens by describing "the Red Ox," the prison in Halle where he had just spent five months:

> In an old university town of my homeland there really is a 'red ox'. Built in the nineteenth century to serve the same purpose which it does today, it is about 1,650 feet long and 1,650 feet wide, and averages 100 feet in height. You can see it from many different vantage points in the city. No one goes willingly into the 'red ox', and once in, one finds it difficult to come out again. Yet thousands of people do live in this old complex of buildings, built in the days of the Prussian kings. These people do not do what they would like, but what they must. They are not happy there. As a general rule they are somewhat depressed. Of those who live there about one hundred hold power over the others. They are obeyed, but there is little joy in this obedience. New men are constantly coming in, but against their wills. Those who have once been inside are desperately afraid of coming in again. You understand, of course, I am speaking of a large prison which, because of its red bricks, has been popularly called the 'red ox' for more than seventy years.[4]

Hamel describes this prison not simply to give his audience an idea of what a prison in East Germany is like, but he goes on to say that "we Christians often turn the Bible into such a 'red ox'". The Bible and its message is misunderstood when they are seen as a rule book, leading those claiming to be Christians to live strained and anxious lives. Those outside the church see this and conclude, as Hamel says, "'The Bible apparently takes all the joy out of living.' So many Christians are for ever trying to make the Bible, which is really a book of joy, into a 'red ox'".[5]

---

4. Hamel, *A Christian in East Germany*, 58.
5. Hamel, *A Christian in East Germany*, 59.

In this address Hamel talks of "concentrated fire;" that is, how Scripture points in a concentrated way to Jesus. From the prophets to the apostles, "(t)he whole sweep of history has had but a single aim, and this goal has now been reached."[6] The result of this concentrated fire is the Pentecost story in which

> a band of messengers comes into being which proclaims the message loudly throughout the world. That this group of heralds should arise is the great miracle of the 'concentrated fire'. The messengers are first the apostles, and then, following them, the Christian community, the *ecclesia*. We usually think that the new thing about the Gospels is their content: that God is merciful, and the he forgives; but really the new thing is first of all the fact that this mercy and forgiveness is said to us, that we can hear it, and that all mankind is assured of it. That is the wonder of it all.[7]

Hamel goes on to compare the gospel to a scene from Beethoven's opera *Fidelio*:

> There lies a man in prison, unjustly confined by the prison's governor. His wife, dressing herself as a soldier, has presented herself for service in the prison. Having been accepted, she looks for a way of saving her husband. In the last scene in the opera catastrophe threatens. The governor has ordered the jailor to behead the prisoner, and the disguised wife has gone with the jailer into the dungeon to prepare for the execution. At the last moment she throws herself between the executioner and her husband, crying, 'I am his wife. You must not kill him!' Just as the answer comes, 'Then you must both die', trumpets are sounded, heralding from afar the coming of the Minister of Justice who will judge fairly and who will free the man. The sound of these trumpets transforms the situation: everything is still as it was; the sword in the hand of the executioner still has the power to kill. But with the trumpets which announce the coming of one

---

6. Hamel, *A Christian in East Germany*, 60.
7. Hamel, *A Christian in East Germany*, 60–61.

who is lord also over the governor, the balance of power has been completely changed. The rescue is there.[8]

Hamel summarizes his understanding of the effect of preaching the gospel:

> We are proclaiming a reality, a reality so immense that the very naming of it basically changes the situation of the hearer, because this is the event of all events. Where the gospel is preached demons are robbed of their power; sins are forgiven; prisoners are freed; and the sorrowing are made joyful: God's wrath is turned to loving-kindness. This and nothing less occurs with the delivery of such a message.[9]

As a pastor, as a teacher, and as a Christian, Hamel's focus is on the centrality of Jesus Christ as Scripture bears witness to him and to the good news of God's grace that he represents. Furthermore, this good news has a present reality that is often lost on those who see the Bible as only a set of rules or who ignore it altogether.

> But what does the Bible say to us today? The Bible speaks only to the present day. The living force speaks only today, for Jesus as (sic) arisen from the dead. Because he lives, his word is always present. In this context we owe a debt of gratitude to Julius Schniewind and Karl Barth, theologians who have opened up for our generation an understanding for the living word of our Lord in the Bible.[10]

In 1950 Hamel wrote a letter to personal friends who lived in the West. Later it was translated and published under the title "God's Beloved East Zone." The title came from a student living in the "East Zone," that is, the German Democratic Republic, who had traveled to the West. He wrote Hamel a letter in which he longed to return to the East. It was not because the student thought that life in the East was necessarily superior to that in the West, but rather

---

8. Hamel, *A Christian in East Germany*, 62.
9. Hamel, *A Christian in East Germany*, 62.
10. Hamel, *A Christian in East Germany*, 66.

he realized that God's gifts were bestowed on those in the East as much as on those in the West. Therefore, he referred to his native country not simply as the "East Zone", but as "God's Beloved East Zone".

In this letter to friends in the West, Hamel notes the greatest need in the East is

> Christ himself, who has performed the miracle for us, that we East Zone people with uneasy and tormented conscience, with all our fear of men and our dull thoughtlessness, with all our envy and bitterness which we wallow in daily, still may belong to him who has not grown weary of us, who still grants us his Word and gathers us to his table."[11]

He notes that many students who are Christians must lead a double life: "on the one side in the Bible Study hour, in public worship, communion and cell group on the other side in the public life of a student."[12] This double life which often leads to internal conflict is illustrated in a university student. Hamel writes:

> So it was with a girl student, who held her ground bravely for a while. She came to know the gospel with wonder and surprise during a long spell in hospital, through the Christian students who visited there, and through it she came to believe. She found in the Christian fellowship her greatest joy; until the day of temptation came. A Communist functionary on the faculty explained to her that she could never expect to be admitted to an examination unless she joined a party. In conscious falsehood she joined the SED (Socialist Unity Party-Communist), and then came to the pastor with the words: 'Now I can no longer participate in the life of the Christian fellowship, because I lie continually.' He pointed out to her that precisely now she needed the comfort of the Word of God, and therefore she ought more than ever to come to the Bible study hour. So she attended both Party

---

11. Hamel, *A Christian in East Germany*, 19.
12. Hamel, *A Christian in East Germany*, 20.

and Christian fellowship, torn in spirit, and ever more miserable.

Hamel continues:

> This is what we Christians are like in the East Zone; and I have only told you a small part of our continual sins of commission and omission. But—and in this 'but' lies the mystery of the living Christ, before whom we can only stand in amazement and shake our heads. But—one day this girl declared to me: 'I can't stand this any longer. I can't pray, I can't read the Bible, I can't take communion. Even if I end up as a charwoman, I won't live with this lie any longer.' So she handed in her resignation to the SED, with such a natural inner peace that it seemed almost a matter of course. That is the greatest miracle, that Christ can and will so draw men to himself, that they become free from themselves, to go their way in his forgiveness with joy, though they can only see the way a yard ahead.

The story does not end there and, according to Hamel, qualifies as another miracle. The student had to appear for a final interview before six functionaries at the SED Party headquarters. Upon being warned that she would lose her scholarship upon which she was completely dependent, she replied, "Because I was afraid for myself, I came to you. Because God has made me free from myself, I am leaving now." Stunned, the functionaries dismissed her. However, one of them commended her privately for her courage. As the examinations approached, the authorities decided that "We must admit this girl. She has sown unusual character in resigning from the Party before the examination time." Hamel concludes with the words, "She passed the examination and suffered no material loss."[13]

Throughout this letter Hamel affirms the presence of God and the Spirit of Jesus Christ in this land in which the government claimed to be atheistic. The church was tolerated, but certainly not encouraged. Indeed, often Christians had to live a double life and

---

13. Hamel, *A Christian in East Germany*, 20–22.

even had to make decisions as to whom they would pay ultimate allegiance.

In the July 10, 1954 issue of the American publication *Presbyterian Life* were a series of conversations Hamel had in 1951 with Marxist university students. In many of these conversations the students were quite committed Marxists, and yet, while unpersuaded by anything Hamel said, left with a newfound respect for Hamel and the way he took them and their positions seriously. Fully aware that any of the students could turn Hamel in to the authorities which could result in his imprisonment, none of them, apparently, did so. Here is an account of one such conversation:

> A fine, strapping young man of twenty-seven years has been sitting with me for the past hour. At nineteen he became a leader in the Hitler Youth, and landed in a Russian war prison. His parents were Nazis. In 1945 they lost their home, house, property, and the father his profession. The family ekes out a poor living as refugees. But the son talks enthusiastically of Russia. 'Think of it! One sixth of humanity already free and prosperous!' He has only good memories of his four years of Russian prison camp: good food, easy chairs, books, sports, discussions in training camps for future functionaries among the German prisoners of war. Of the experiences of others he will hear nothing in his heaven-storming idealism. Now he works enthusiastically for the Party. Whoever doesn't join in the fight for peace is, for him, a warmonger. When I referred to the real situation in Russia, his young voice took on a threatening undertone: 'That is incitement against the Soviet Union.' Such remarks are not exactly pleasant in the mouth of a Communist. Should he denounce me, it could mean many years at forced labour. I tried everything possible to find a common language with him. In the question of the rearming of Germany (which I oppose for both East and West), I pointed to our East German People's Police, which drills every day like infantry with military shovels. He denied it. 'But,' I cried, 'my own eyes see it. A troop of them marches by every day on its way to the training ground. That's no mere police squad, that's infantry.' Finally he got excited:

> 'You are always talking about your eyes, and about the real situation. You must first analyse the thing scientifically, and then you will know what the People's Police in its essence is.'

Hamel admitted mutual frustration that no common ground could be found in this conversation. When he observed that all East Germans lived in fear of being arrested, "he laughed out loud and called me an other-worldly fool. When I put it to him that no one would dare to speak the truth to him as soon as they recognized him on the street as a Communist functionary, he was shaken, but he denied it vehemently." Finally, the two parted ways, Hamel sensing that he had probably driven his conversation partner "deeper into his ideological shell, instead of luring him out." Hamel concluded with the question, "What must lie beneath, in this one-time Nazi enthusiast, that he so loses himself in a blind belief, that he puts more faith in Lenin's theories than in what he sees with his own eyes?"[14]

On October 26, 1955 Hamel delivered a remarkable lecture entitled, "The Courage to be Truthful" to students at the University of Leipzig. After reviewing the parable of Hans Christian Andersen's fairy tale, "The Emperor's New Clothes," in which only a child has the audacity to declare that, while the adults are fawning over the invisible clothes of the emperor, he is actually wearing no clothes at all, Hamel explores the complexities of telling the truth. Are there times when it is acceptable not to tell the truth? Are there times when one has the license to lie? Whether physician, journalist, politician, spouse, parent, or child, Hamel maintains, one most certainly has been in a position of deceiving another person. From this perspective, telling the truth is a complicated matter.

But then Hamel makes a crucial move by asserting that the question "What is the truth?" is the wrong question: "Truth is nothing. God himself is the truth, and this truth became man in Jesus Christ. This one who embodies truth "has made its home among us liars." Our relationship to this one who is the Truth is one in which we flee, we lie, we deny, we reject, we mock. The

---

14. Hamel, *A Christian in East Germany*, 39–41.

remarkable thing is that instead of rejecting us, instead of "annihilating" those who reject him, he calls them to repent and "rescues all those who call upon his name. The truth makes us free!"'"[15]

To live as a truthful person is to praise and honor God. "Not to praise God every day ... is to lie," Hamel writes.[16] He then goes on to ask what that means for someone who lives in the German Democratic Republic. One of the risks persons of faith run in that environment is that of thinking themselves better "than those who oppress us." Hamel puts the issue in perspective by asking, "(W)ill God ask us about the evil deeds of others in the Last Judgment, or will he ask us what we have done and what we deserve? We cannot wash ourselves clean with the evil of others."[17] In fact, he says,

> As messengers of Jesus we must testify, to men who know no peace, of the peace which God has made with us all. We must make God's compassion credible to those who hate God. We should make it easier for the distrustful nihilists and cynics to trust our heavenly Father: we should make it easier for the atonement to speak to the heart of the hate-filled fanatic.[18]

Clearly, Hamel's perspective reflects one that is distinct from any political or ideological framework. His starting point is that of his understanding of the gospel and how that understanding informs everyday life and relationships with others. The Christian life and the Christian understanding of truth are characterized by love. Therefore,

> (t)he people about us are not given to us so that we may hate them and battle with them. We should neither be indifferent to them nor be afraid of them ... To love means that we look at and honour our actual neighbour as the man who carries God's image; that we accept and receive him as one for whom Jesus Christ gave up his life.[19]

15. Hamel, *A Christian in East Germany*, 92.
16. Hamel, *A Christian in East Germany*, 93.
17. Hamel, *A Christian in East Germany*, 94–95.
18. Hamel, *A Christian in East Germany*, 95.
19. Hamel, *A Christian in East Germany* 97.

Furthermore, Hamel maintains that the Christian is neither pro-Marxist nor anti-Marxist. This does not mean that one is either silent or passive towards the political realities in one's own life.

Rather, it means that one recognize and acknowledge the flaws in any and all human ideologies and institutions. He writes:

> When a Christian refused perhaps to declare his adherence to views of dialectical and historical materialism, with their economic and political consequences, he does not do it as a follower of any kind of anti-Marxism. The assertion that there is only friend or enemy has no justification under the Lordship of truth . . . We are not Bolshevists, but neither are we anti-Bolshevists. As Jesus' messengers we are there for our neighbours. We are never their enemies.[20]

Hamel concludes this lecture to East German university students in Leipzig with a challenge for Christians and for the church:

> Only a few decades ago nothing was more boring than the Church and its message. Today we live in another age: truth is demanded of us; we should rejoice in this even in the midst of our distress. 'God's word cannot be proclaimed without uproar,' says Luther. God always has great plans for his Christians when he sends such 'uproar'. The free word of truth wants, demands, to be spoken forth, in everyday life and work, by no means first of all from the pulpit. Let us guard against forgetting this good school of God's.[21]

In August 1958 Karl Barth wrote a letter in response to eight questions posed by a pastor living in "the German East Zone." The following year Barth's letter with a response from Hamel and an essay by Hamel appeared under the title *How to Serve God in a Marxist Land*.[22] At the time some wondered why Barth had re-

---

20. Hamel, *A Christian in East Germany* 99–100.

21. Hamel, *A Christian in East Germany* 101.

22. It is not clear to this writer who wrote the original letter to which Barth responds. In his response to Barth, Hamel writes: "Last October you wrote a letter to us pastors in East Germany." Did Hamel write the original letter

mained comparatively silent on the oppression of the church in communist countries when he had been so outspoken about the evils of Nazism only a couple of decades before. Noteworthy among these critics was Reinhold Niebuhr, at the time professor at Union Theological Seminary in New York. Barth's response to this criticism lies, in part, in the fact that he must be as critical of the West and its values as he is of the East. If the East is, at best, indifferent to the church and, at worst, hostile toward it, then the West, according to Barth,

> seeks to dissuade the Christian Church from being the church. It attempts to silence the fearless, resounding proclamation so alien and so disturbing to the world, that God's rule is close at hand and will ultimately be revealed to the whole earth, that his kingdom is supreme and victorious over all economic, political, ideological, cultural, and also religious realms of life.[23]

Throughout Barth's letter one finds the phrase "*God above all things!*" This theme appears to be his starting point. The church's task is not "to rebut a materialistic world-view with a Christian world-view . . . Only 'firm in the faith,' that is in *this* faith, can the church resist; never, in the name or in honor of any principles or dogmas, in an attempt to compel anyone to recognize them in theory or practice. She can only follow Jesus."[24] Before addressing the specific questions raised in the original letter to him, Barth writes that "(w)hat you and we must fear and love above all things is not any abstract idea, theory, deity, or law, but God's free grace alone, eternally sovereign and revealed to us in Jesus Christ."[25]

---

to Barth, or was it a letter sent on behalf of several pastors? Robert McAfee Brown, who translated the correspondence and wrote an introductory essay, apparently, believes that Hamel was the author of the initial letter (see "Good News from Karl Barth" in *How Karl Barth Changed My Mind*, 95). Interestingly, in his letter Barth refers to Hamel in the third person when he (Barth) mentions a paper by Hamel that appears at the end of this volume is considered at the end of this chapter.

23. Barth and Hamel, *How to Serve God in a Marxist Land*, 51–52.
24. Barth and Hamel, *How to Serve God in a Marxist Land*, 60.
25. Barth and Hamel, *How to Serve God in a Marxist Land*, 61.

Following this 21-page message, Barth does address the eight specific questions that are posed by this East German pastor. One of the questions deals with the matter of loyalty: "Can we pledge the required loyalty oath to the East German government, in spite of the inherent dangers?" While acknowledging that he does not know the exact wording of this loyalty oath, Barth offers the following thoughts:

> "Loyalty" does *not* mean approval of the ideology on which this government is built. It does not mean approval of each and every measure of the actual officials and representatives of this government. "Loyalty" reserves the right of freedom of thought over against the ideology, and the right of opposition, even of resistance to particular implications and applications of the given system. There is such a thing as a loyal opposition . . .[26]

Hamel responds, apparently on behalf of a number of pastors, to Barth's letter. He says he writes "to express a hearty word of thanks to you, our fatherly teacher and friend" and notes that he has spoken "to many of my colleagues in the pastorate and in teaching" whom Barth's letter has "comforted, strengthened, and exhorted," and at the same time "also warned . . . of this and that abyss, that we may rightly fight the good fight of the faith and hold fast unto him who has won the victory."[27]

Hamel goes on to write:

> All of us who received your letter are engaged in a difficult struggle for the freedom of the gospel on two fronts: against our own evil, lazy, and loveless heart; and against a massive outside attack on faith, witness, and obedience. With earnestness, urgency, and relaxed humor you invite us in this inward and outward struggle to hold fast unto the Lord who has loved the godless people we are, and has embraced in his love for the world also.[28]

---

26. Barth and Hamel, *How to Serve God in a Marxist Land*, 68.
27. Barth and Hamel, *How to Serve God in a Marxist Land*, 81–82.
28. Barth and Hamel, *How to Serve God in a Marxist Land*, 82.

Hamel continues his description of the effect of Barth's letter on East German pastors with these words:

> Best of all, your letter gives us courage to read the Bible, to preach, to bear witness, and to make free decisions. The unhindered proclamation of the gospel in the Marxist world and the joyful obedience amidst a world that likes to display atheism—certainly a painstaking and risky task, desperate driving to despair—are strengthened and affirmed in your letter.[29]

The last article by Hamel that we will consider here is one that is titled "The Proclamation of the Gospel in the Marxist World." Barth refers to it in his letter and indicates that the article was a contribution to a Festschrift honoring Eduard Thurneysen, Barth's friend and colleague. In this essay Hamel addresses what he considers to be the fundamental question: "Does the Christian Church in the Marxist world hear and acknowledge her own gospel in its sovereignty and in all its dimensions? . . . Or does the Christian Church understand the powers which rule over her on the basis of a stereotype of ecclesiastical, political, social, and cultural traditions?" He poses the question in another way: "Does the Christian Church deny the total sovereignty of the gospel of God over everything in heaven and on earth? . . . Or does the Christian Church proclaim publicly and privately, in small and great things, that all powers and principalities are already overcome and imprisoned through the resurrection of Jesus Christ?"[30]

After asking "What does it mean to accept the Marxist world in the light of the gospel?" Hamel proceeds to biblical examples of times when Israel faced life under foreign powers: the Assyrians in the eighth century BCE, the Babylonians in the late seventh and early sixth century BCE, the Persians in the sixth century BCE,

---

29. Barth and Hamel, *How to Serve God in a Marxist Land*, 83. It is worth noting that this was not the only exchange of letters between Barth and Hamel. On August 19, 1963 Barth responded to a letter from Hamel having to do with the "Ten Articles on the Freedom and Service of the Church" which was adopted at a conference of church leaders in East Germany. Barth's letter can be found in Karl Barth, *Letters, 1961-1968*, 122-23.

30. Barth and Hamel, *How to Serve God in a Marxist Land*, 85-6.

and, finally, the Romans in the life of the early church in the late first and early second century CE. He writes:

> In these periods of history the people of God had to face the question as to whether or not the indicated reactions, real or possible, to submission under Assyria, Babylonia, Persia, and the Roman emperor represented the final word of wisdom. Was their action always to be dictated by either revolt or alignment? The preaching of Isaiah, Jeremiah, the unknown preacher in the middle of the sixth century (Isaiah 40–55), and the summaries of the early church's proclamation in various parts of the New Testament, all deny this either/or alternative. Neither do they propagate a middle line between the two extremes. (This was the attitude of the Pharisaic party up to the Jewish war!). The prophets reach down to a deeper level and proclaim these bearers of new power and order to be the instruments of Israel's Lord who created the universe.[31]

Hamel cites Romans 13 and Revelation 13 as illustrations of how the early church faced and dealt with living under a hostile foreign power. He also looks at Jesus's words in the Passion stories, namely, the confrontation between the priests and Jesus and Pontius Pilate and Jesus, and how the priests and Pilate were considered to be "instruments of God's mercy and compassion as he [God] deals with the world."[32]

Hamel's argument is that, regardless of how adverse the circumstances, the people of God are to remember who they are and whose they are and that, as such, they are to be a part of the society in which they live and to be active in public affairs. He points to Jeremiah's letter to his fellow Jews in Jeremiah 29:5–7:

> Build houses and live in them; plant gardens and eat their produce. Take wives and have sons and daughters; take wives for your sons, and give your daughters in marriage, that they may bear sons and daughters; multiply there, and do not decrease. But seek the welfare of the

---

31. Hamel, *How to Serve God in a Marxist Land*, 1.
32. Hamel, *How to Serve God in a Marxist Land*, 93.

city where I have sent you into exile, and pray to the Lord on its behalf, for in its welfare you will find your welfare.

It would be a mistake, Hamel maintains, to wish one were somewhere else, for God can be praised and obeyed wherever one is. In addition, the issues elsewhere may be different, but no less onerous than where one lives. Referring to his own contemporary situation, Hamel observes that, as difficult as life can be under communist rule, it is also the case that in the Soviet Union, for example, there was "remarkable growth" in the Orthodox Church there. His point is that "(w)e must desist once and for all from placing Christianity and its teaching into the strait jacket of Christian anti-communism or pro-communism."[33]

To think of Marxism as good or bad, he argues,

> is a denial of the gospel if it becomes our primary concern . . . The gospel makes us free people who do not rebel against the visitation of God calling us to repentance by sending us these servants. The gospel releases us from bitter silence and from glorifying gossip. It looses our tongues for the praise of God whose majesty draws into his service even Marxism and the Marxists.[34]

Even in a Marxist country one is, as Paul says, "subject to the governing authorities." That does not mean that one must agree with those authorities. For Christians, it simply means that, one's ultimate allegiance is to God. The temptation may be to think that "Marxist power has won the day while God remains silent." Hamel continues:

> There are those in the church who rise to a positive appreciation of Marxism. They discover a philosophy of history which recognizes in Marxism the new era for the good of humanity. It sways the future while the "West" stumbles toward its grave. But others rise against them. In angry indignation they attack everything which is incompatible with the conception of a law-abiding state. For them it is of the essence of Christian faith to

---

33. Hamel, *How to Serve God in a Marxist Land*, 102.
34. Hamel, *How to Serve God in a Marxist Land*, 105–6.

oppose Marxism and to condemn it as immoral and irreligious.[35]

Hamel maintains that both positions are misguided because each has substituted a worldview for the gospel. Each position subordinates the gospel to an ideological perspective. If it is true that God is active and involved in the lives of people in spite of living under a Marxist regime, then it is also true that God can be active and involved in the lives of people living under a capitalist democratic system of government. In other words, both systems are flawed, and both can misrepresent, manipulate, or even deny the gospel. However, that does not diminish the power of the gospel to influence the affairs of people and nations. The church in both East and West must be confronted with the scandal of the gospel that condemns and frees all points-of-view that claim a moral high road and that judges others.

Toward the end of this essay Hamel reiterates this theme:

> The gospel puts things in their place, it gives us sound eyes gratefully to see justice, freedom, humanity, peace, and order as God's good gifts, provided in the Marxist realm. We must point out these positive things because we are assured by God's promise that he will not desert his creation, that he will not cause another flood to come.[36]

This statement reflects a willingness on the part of a Christian pastor to labor within a system that is not only unsympathetic to religion, in general, and Christianity, in particular, but engages in activities to undermine its effectiveness. One might ask why one would not openly resist this system of government. By committing himself to the gospel first, Hamel suggests that that is a form of resistance. But by committing himself to the gospel first, Hamel also affirms a higher allegiance to it than to the government.

---

35. Hamel, *How to Serve God in a Marxist Land*, 107. Hanfried Müller is an example of the former, while Reinhold Niebuhr, among others, would be an example of the latter.

36. Hamel, *How to Serve God in a Marxist Land*, 120.

It is also important to note that Hamel, like Barth, suffers no illusion that life in the West does not have its own issues that might be considered as egregious or dangerous as those in the East. The West can suffer both from a sense of complacency and comfort that comes with the freedoms afforded by its democratic institutions and from a smug self-righteousness that can undermine, if it does not deny, the scandal of the gospel that transcends nationalism and forms of government. The gospel has no favorite form of government. From a theological point-of-view, regardless of how free or how oppressive a government may be, one is guided, first and foremost, by the dictum *"God above all things!"* as Barth (and Hamel) affirm.

CHAPTER 6

Conclusion

LIVING UNDER AN AUTHORITARIAN, let alone a totalitarian form of government, must be difficult for most persons. Living under Communist rule must also be difficult for many, if not most, persons. Living as a committed Christian under Communist rule was a particular struggle. This was true in the former East Germany as well as elsewhere. Hanfried Müller was not only sympathetic with but was an enthusiastic supporter of the East German Marxist regime. For him, a Christian theologian, Marxist ideology was the best political expression by which people could and should be governed. As has been seen, Müller's commitment to Marxist ideology not only informed, but superseded his theology, so much so that he served as a secret informant for the East German government.

In contrast, for Johannes Hamel (and many other pastors, theologians, and church leaders), the gospel came first. That commitment to the gospel created a necessary and healthy distance—or separation—between the church and the state. It enabled the church to engage the state without becoming enmeshed with it. Hamel and others acknowledged the biblical injunction to "be subject to the governing authorities" (Romans 13:1) and to "honor the emperor" (1 Peter 2:17), but they also affirmed the role and place of the church. This relationship is best articulated in the

Conclusion

Theological Declaration of Barmen, written principally by Karl Barth and adopted by the Confessing Church in May 1934. In Article 5 one finds: "We reject the false doctrine, as though the State, over and beyond its special commission, should and could become the single and totalitarian order of human life, thus fulfilling the church's vocation as well."

Immediately following those words one comes upon these: "We reject the false doctrine, as though the church, over and beyond its special commission, should and could appropriate the characteristics, the tasks, and the dignity of the State, thus itself becoming an organ of the State."[1] This theological declaration acknowledges the important and necessary role of both the church and the state, but neither presuming to assume the role of the other. Nothing is said about the form of either the church or the state.

For the purposes of this study it is equally important to note that this same theological declaration, composed initially in the early stages of the church struggle against the Nazi regime, addresses the matter of ideology. In Article 3 we read: "We reject the false doctrine, as though the church were permitted to abandon the form of its message and order to its own pleasure or to changes in prevailing ideological and political convictions."[2] This would seem to apply directly to the thought of Hanfried Müller who subordinates his theological convictions to his political and ideological convictions.

While this work might be seen as a case study contrasting two very different theological perspectives, it is hoped that it will be seen as much more than that. First, it has provided a way of emphasizing the importance of one's starting point in theology. For Müller, his Marxist convictions became his point of departure. For Hamel, and many others, God is above all things and the confession that Jesus is Lord overrode everything else. Their starting points were crucial in determining the trajectory of their theology.

Second, these two perspectives say something about their understanding of power. For Müller, by participating in the power of

1. "Theological Declaration of Barmen," paragraphs 8.23 and 8.24.
2. "Theological Declaration of Barmen," paragraph 8.18.

the state over the role of the church, he placed himself on the side of the state against the church. On the other hand, Hamel and many who served as pastors, theological faculty members, and church officials, while subject to the laws and actions of the state, affirmed the church's independence from the state and drew strength from the power of the Spirit which enabled them to engage in the work and ministry of the church.

Third, this study is instructive beyond the life of the church "beyond the wall." Hamel and his colleagues have provided an example of how one can struggle but still be effective in extremely adverse situations. The focus of Hamel's attention was on the gospel and "God above all things!" That enabled him to overcome discouragement and to concentrate on what was most important, vocationally, and to be reminded by Barth that, while there may be more freedom in the West, the way of life in the West was not without its own flaws and shortcomings. Effective ministry can happen anywhere, even in authoritarian and totalitarian countries.

The end of Communist rule in eastern Europe did not lead to an end of authoritarian governments. Although Germany experienced a reunification under a parliamentary democracy, and while many countries previously under the rule of the former Soviet Union achieved independence, there are many places where the church is suppressed and oppressed. Johannes Hamel and his colleagues offer courageous examples of what life and ministry might look like in those circumstances.

Bibliography

Altizer, Thomas J. J. and William Hamilton. *Radical Theology and the Death of God*. Indianapolis: Bobbs–Merrill, 1966.
Arendt, Hannah. *The Origins of Totalitarianism*. Cleveland: World, 1958.
Ash, Timothy Garton. *The Magic Lantern: The Revolution of '89 Witnessed in Warsaw, Budapest, Berlin, and Prague*. New York: Random House, 1990.
"Aus der negativen Kreuzestheologie keine negative Weltanschauung machen. Gespräch mit Hanfried Müller (Ost-Berlin)." *Kreuz & Quer* 2 (1991) 12–20.
Badstübner, Rolf, ed. *Geschichte der Deutschen Demokratischen Republik*. Berlin: VEB Deutscher Verlag der Wissenschaften, 1981.
Bark, Dennis L. and David R. Gress. *A History of West Germany*. Oxford: Blackwell, 1993.
Barth, Karl. *Action in Waiting*. Rifton, New York: Plough, 1969.
———. *Against the Stream: Shorter Post-War Writings, 1946–52*. London: SCM, 1954.
———. *Church and State*. Greenville, SC: Smyth Helwys, 1991.
———. *Church Dogmatics*. Edinburgh: T. & T. Clark.
———. *The Epistle to the Romans*. London: Oxford University Press, 1975.
———. *How I Changed My Mind*. Richmond: John Knox, 1966.
———. *Karl Barth-Eduard Thurneysen Briefwechsel, 1913–1921*. Zürich: Theologischer Verlag, 1973.
———. *The Word of God and the Word of Man*. Gloucester: Peter Smith, 1978.
Barth, Karl and Johannes Hamel. *How to Serve God in a Marxist Land*. New York: Association, 1959.
Beeson, Trevor. *Discretion and Valour: Religious Conditions in Russia and Eastern Europe*. Philadelphia: Fortress, 1982.
Beintker, Michael. "Die Idee des Friedens als Waffe im Kalten Krieg." *Kirchliche Zeitgeschichte* 4 (1991) 249–59.
———. "Die Schuldfrage im Erfahrungsfeld des gesellschaftlichen Umbruchs im östlichen Deutschland." *Kirchliche Zeitgeschichte* 4 (1992), 445–61.
———. "Nachdenkliche Rückblenden auf das Verhältnis von Kirche und Staat in der DDR." *Kirchliche Zeitgeschichte* 7 (1994), 300–18.

BIBLIOGRAPHY

Bentley, James. *Between Marx and Christ: The Dialogue in German-Speaking Europe, 1870-1970.* London: NLB, 1982.

Berger, Wolfgang. "Zu den Hauptursachen des Unterganges der DDR." *Weißenseer Blätter* 4 (1992) 26-36, 71.

Berlin, Isaiah. *Karl Marx: His Life and Environment.* New York: Time, 1963.

Besier, Gerhard. *Der SED-Staat und die Kirche, 1969-1990.* Berlin: Propyläen, 1995.

Besier, Gerhard und Stephan Wolf, eds. *"Pfarrer, Christen und Katholiken": Das Ministerium für Staatssicherheit der ehemaligen DDR und die Kirchen.* Neukirchen-Vluyn: Neukirchner, 1991.

Bethge, Eberhard. "Besprechung. Hanfried Müller: *Von der Kirche zur Welt.* Ein Beitrag zu der Beziehung des Wortes Gottes auf die Societas in Dietrich Bonhoeffers theologischer Entwicklung." *Die mündige Welt* 4 (1963) 169-74.

———. *Dietrich Bonhoeffer: Man of Vision, Man of Courage.* New York: Harper & Row, 1970.

Boer, Dick. "Kann man 'die DDR vergessen . . . '?" *Weißenseer Blätter* 3 (1993) 34-38.

Bonhoeffer, Dietrich. *Act and Being.* New York: Harper & Row, 1962.

———. *The Cost of Discipleship.* New York: Macmillan, 1963.

———. *Ethics.* New York: Macmillan, 1955.

———. *Letters and Papers from Prison.* New York: Macmillan, 1971.

———. *Sanctorum Communio: A Dogmatic Inquiry into the Sociology of the Church.* London: Collins, 1963.

Bracher, Karl Dietrich. *The Age of Ideologies: A History of Political Thought in the Twentieth Century.* New York: St. Martin's, 1984.

———. *The German Dictatorship: The Origins, Structure, and Effects of National Socialism.* New York: Praeger, 1970.

———. *The German Dilemma: The Throes of Political Emancipation.* London: Weidenfeld and Nicolson, 1974.

———. *Turning Points in Modern Times: Essays on German and European History.* Cambridge, MA: Harvard University Press, 1995.

———. *Zeitgeschichtliche Kontroversen um Faschismus, Totalitarismus, Demokratie.* München: R. Piper, 1976.

Bracher, Karl Dietrich, et al., eds. *Deutschland 1933-1945: Neue Studien zur nationalsozialistischen Herrschaft.* Düsseldorf: Droste, 1992.

Breipohl, Renate. *Religiöser Sozialismus und bürgerliches Geschichtsbesußtsein zur Zeit der Weimarer Republik.* Zürich: Theologischer Verlag, 1971.

"Briefwechsel über ein Buch . . . zwischen Gerneralsuperintendent i. R. Dr. Horst Lahr und Prof. Dr. sc. Hanfried Müller." *Standpunkt* (1980) 187-93.

Burgess, John P. "Christian Political Involvement in East and West: The Theological Ethics of Wolf Krötke." *The Journal of Religion* 71 (1991) 202-16.

———. "Church-State Relations in East Germany: The Church as a 'Religious' and 'Political' Force." *Journal of Church and State* 32 (1990) 17-35.

BIBLIOGRAPHY

———. *The East German Church and the End of Communism*. New York: Oxford University Press, 1997.

———. "Preparing for the Fall of 1989: Religion and Democratization in East Germany." *Soundings* 74 (1991) 45–64.

———. "Stolpe and the Stasi." *Christian Century* (1992) 1124–26.

Burtness, James. *Shaping the Future: The Ethics of Dietrich Bonhoeffer*. Philadelphia: Fortress, 1985.

Busch, Eberhard. *Karl Barth: His Life from Letters and Autobiographical Texts*. Philadelphia: Fortress, 1976.

Collingwood, R. G. *The Idea of History*. New York: Oxford University Press, 1956.

Cone, James H. *Black Theology & Black Power*. New York: Seabury, 1969.

Conway, John S. "Kirche im Sozialismus: East German Protestantism's Political and Theological Witness, 1945–1990." *Religion in Eastern Europe* 13 (1993) 1–21.

Cort, John C. *Christian Socialism: An Informal History*. Maryknoll: Orbis, 1988.

Dähn, Horst, ed. *Die Rolle der Kirchen in der DDR*. München: Olzog, 1993.

Day, Thomas I. "Essay Review." *Union Seminary Quarterly Review* 28 (1972) 117–21.

DeGruchy, John W., ed., *Bonhoeffer and South Africa: Theology in Dialogue*. Grand Rapids, MI: Eerdmans, 1984.

Deschner, John W. "Karl Barth as Political Activist." *Union Seminary Quarterly Review* 28 (1972) 55–66.

Dierse, Ulrich. "Ideologie." In *Geschichtliche Grundbegriffe: Historisches Lexikon zu politisch-sozialen Sprache in Deutschland*. Stuttgart: Ernst Klett, 1982.

Dill, Marshall, Jr. *Germany: A Modern History*. Ann Arbor: University of Michigan Press, 1961.

Ebert, Andreas, et al., eds. *Räumt die Steine himweg. DDR Herbst Geistliche Reden im politischen Aufbruch*. Ingolstadt: Claudius, 1989.

Fangmeier, Jürgen and Hinrich Stoevesandt, eds. *Karl Barth Letters, 1961–1968*. Grand Rapids, MI: Eerdmans, 1981.

Feil, Ernst. *The Theology of Dietrich Bonhoeffer*. Philadelphia: Fortress, 1985.

Feuerbach, Ludwig. *The Essence of Christianity*. Translated by George Eliot. New York: Harper & Row, 1957.

Forstman, Jack. *Christian Faith in Dark Times: Theological Conflicts in the Shadow of Hitler*. Louisville: Westminster/John Knox, 1992.

Frielinghaus, Dieter. "Kirche in der Wendezeit." *Weißenseer Blätter* 3 (1990) 3–8.

———. "Wir haben uns nicht geirrt in unserem Einsatz für den Sozialismus." *Weißenseer Blätter* 4 (1990) 3–10.

Goeckel Robert F. "The Evangelical-Lutheran Church and the East German Revolution." *Occasional Papers on Religion in Eastern Europe* 10 (1990) 28–43.

BIBLIOGRAPHY

———. *The Lutheran Church and the East German State: Political Conflict and Change under Ulbricht and Honecker*. Ithaca: Cornell University Press, 1990.

Grabner, Jürgen, et al., eds. *Leipzig im Oktober*. Berlin: Wichern, 1990.

Green, Clifford. *Bonhoeffer: The Sociality of Christ and Humanity*. Missoula: Scholars, 1989.

———. *Karl Barth: Theologian of Freedom*. London: Collins Liturgical, 1989.

Gutierrez, Gustavo. *A Theology of Liberation: History, Politics, and Salvation*. Maryknoll: Orbis, 1973.

Hamel, Johannes. *A Christian in East Germany*. Translated by Ruth and Charles C. West. Naperville: SCM, 1960.

Hanisch, Günter, et al., eds. *Dona nobis pacem. Fürbitten und Friedensgebete Herbst '89 in Leipzig*. Berlin: Evangelische Verlagsanstalt, 1990.

Henry, David. "Lutheran pastor, Christian Führer, East German dissident, dies at 71." *The Washington Post* (July 1, 2014). https://www.washingtonpost.com/world/europe/lutheran-pastor-christian-fuhrer-east-german-dissident-dies-at-71/2014/07/01/d9f67cc2-0131-11e4-8572-4b1b969b6322_story.html?utm_term=.a2304cddd31f

Huber, Wolfgang, ed. *Protestanten in der Demokratie. Positionen und Profile im Nachkriegsdeutschland*. München: Christian Kaiser, 1990.

Hunsinger, George, ed. *Karl Barth and Radical Politics*. Philadelphia: Westminster, 1976.

Jüngel, Eberhard. "Barth, Karl." In *Theologische Realenzyklopädie*. Band V. Berlin: Walter de Gruyter, 1980.

———. *Karl Barth: A Theological Legacy*. Translated by Garrett E. Paul. Philadelphia: Westminster, 1986.

"Klarheit in den großen Fragen. Gespräch Günter Wirths mit Prof. Hanfried Müller." *Standpunkt* (1974) 169–70.

Krötke, Wolf. "Karl Barths und Dietrich Bonhoeffers Bedeutung für die Theologie in der DDR." *Kirchliche Zeitgeschichte* 7 (1994) 279–99.

Krusche, Günther. "A New Learning Process Has Begun: The Church in a Post-Socialist Society." *Occasional Papers on Religion in Eastern Europe* 10 (1990) 44–49.

Krusche, Werner. *Und Gott redete mit seinem Volk. Predigten aus den achtziger Jahren*. Stuttgart: Calwer, 1990.

Laqueur, Walter. *Europe in Our Time: A History, 1945–1992*. New York: Viking Penguin, 1992.

Lehmann, Paul. "Karl Barth, Theologian of Permanent Revolution." *Union Seminary Quarterly Review* 28 (1972) 67–81.

Leith, John H., ed. *Creeds of the Churches: A Reader in Christian Doctrine from the Bible to the Present*. Atlanta: John Knox, 1982.

Linke, Dietmar. *Theologiestudenten der Humboldt-Universität. Zwischen Hörsaal und Anklagebank*. Neukirchen-Vluyn: Neukirchener, 1994.

Mann, Golo. *The History of Germany Since 1789*. New York: Praeger, 1968.

BIBLIOGRAPHY

Marquardt, Friedrich-Wilhelm. *Theologie und Sozialismus. Das Beispiel Karl Barths*. München: Chr. Kaiser, 1972.

Marx, Karl. *The Communist Manifesto*. New York: International, 1948.

———. *On Religion*. The Karl Marx Library 5. New York: McGraw-Hill, 1974.

Marx, Karl and Frederick Engels. *Collected Works Volume 3*. New York: International, 1975.

Massanari, Ronald L. "Christian Socialism in Nineteenth Century Germany: A Case Study of a Shift in Anthropological Perspective." *Union Seminary Quarterly Review* 29 (1973) 17–25.

McCauley, Martin. "East Germany: The Dilemmas of Division." *Conflict Studies* 119 (1980) 1–19.

———. *The German Democratic Republic since 1945*. New York: St. Martin's Press, 1983.

Mosse, George. *The Crisis of German Ideology: Intellectual Origins of the Third Reich*. New York: Grosset & Dunlap, 1964.

———. *Nazi Culture: Intellectual, Cultural and Social Life in the Third Reich*. New York: Grosset & Dunlap, 1966.

Müller, Hanfried. "Anschauung der zersplitterten Welt und zersplitterte Weltanschauung." *Weißenseer Blätter* 1 (1993) 17–22.

———. "Barmen—Selbstrechtfertigung der Kirche?" *Standpunkt* (1984) 183–84.

———. "Barth und Barmen. Eine wichtige Dokumentation." *Standpunkt* 54–55.

———. "Der Christ in Kirche und Staat." Edited by Otto Nuschke in connection with the Party Leadership of Christlich-Demokratischen Union. Zentralen Schulungsstätte, 1958.

———. "Der christlich-marxistische Dialog. Gedanken und Bedenken." *Die Weißenseer Blätter* 3 (1993) 13–21.

———. "Der 'Fall Stolpe' und die Sicherheit der Demokratie." *Weißenseer Blätter* 2 (1992) 51–53.

———. "Der Kirchenkampf—Reformation im 20. Jahrhundert." *Standpunkt* (1984) 20–24.

———. "Der tragische Stoff in der sozialistischen Gesellschaft. Ein Fragment aus dem Jahr 1955." *Weißenseer Blätter* 1 (1985) 42–50.

———. "Die Begegnung evangelischer Theologie mit dem historisch-dialektischen Materialismus—Holzweg? Irrweg? Wegerkundigung? Eine Apologie." *Weißenseer Blätter* 4 (1991) 15–29; 5 (1991) 46–62; 1 (1992) 44–48; 2 (1992) 12–28; 5 (1992) 50–62.

———. "Die Verantwortung der Kirche als Siegermacht." *Weißenseer Blätter* 1 (1990) 6–10.

———. "Dietrich Bonhoeffer—Christuszeuge in der Bekennenden Kirche für die mündige Welt." *Dietrich Bonhoeffer—Kämpfer gegen Krieg und Faschismus*. Berlin: Beiträge zur Geschichte der Humboldt-Universität, 1981. (This article also appears in *Standpunkt* (1981) 90–92, and in

BIBLIOGRAPHY

Bonhoeffer-Studien, listed below under Schönherr, Albrecht and Wolf Krötke.)

———. "Einige Theologische Randbemerkungen zu einigen heimlichen Dogmen unserer Kirche." *Weißenseer Blätter* 2 (1990) 6–9.

———. *Evangelische Dogmatik im Überblick* 2 Bände. Berlin: Evangelische Verlagsanstalt, 1978.

———. "Geschichte, Kirchengeschichte und Historiographie. Kritisches und Polemisches zu Scholders 'Die Kirchen und das Dritte Reich.'" *Standpunkt* (1978) 189–92, 216–19.

———. "Gratulation eines Außenseiters zum 175. Geburtstag von Karl Marx." *Weißenseer Blätter* 2 (1993) 30–54.

———. "Hromadka." *Standpunkt* (1978) 163.

———. "Kirche im Revolutionären Weltprozess. Kirche im Sozialismus. Thesen." *Weißenseer Blätter* 4 (1983) 12–14.

———. "Militärische Kirchenpolitik und kirchliche Militärpolitik in den deutschen evangelischen Kirchen gegenüber der Bundeswehr NVA." *Weißenseer Blätter* 3 (1983) 26–34.

———. "Offener Brief an meine Freunde in der SED." *Weißenseer Blätter* 5 (1989) 25–38.

———. "Randbemerkungen zu einigen Randerscheinungen zwischen Kirche und Kulture." *Weißenseer Blätter* 4 (1982) 37–47; 1 (1983) 20–32.

———. "Reflexionen zur Freiheit am Tag der Befreiung." *Standpunkt* (1975) 114–16.

———. *Von der Kirche zur Welt. Ein Beitrag zu der Beziehung des Wortes Gottes auf die Societas in Dietrich Bonhoeffers theologischer Entwicklung.* Hamburg–Bergsted: Herbert Reich Evangel, 1961.

———. "Warum ich im Ernstfall für den Kommunismus votiere." *Weißenseer Blätter* 7 (1988) 10–31.

———. "'Zusammenbruch' und/oder 'Konterrevolution.'" *Weißenseer Blätter* 4 (1992) 57–68.

Müller, Hanfried and Rosemarie Müller-Streisand. "Stuttgart 1945 und 1975." *Standpunkt* (1975) 225–28.

Nielsen, Niels. *Revolutions in Eastern Europe*. Maryknoll: Orbis, 1991.

Onnasch, Martin. "Konflikt und Kompromiß. Die Haltung der evangelischen Kirchen zu den gesellschaftlichen Veränderungen in der DDR am Anfang der fünfziger Jahre." *Kirchliche Zeitgeschichte* 3 (1990) 152–65.

Pasztor, Janos. "Hermann Kutter: Pioneer Social Theologian, 1863–1931." *The Princeton Seminary Bulletin* 65 (1972) 80–87.

———. "Leonard Ragaz: Pioneer Social Theologian." *Union Seminary Quarterly Review* 29 (1973) 27–33.

Pierard, Richard V. "Editorial—Religion and the East German Revolution." *Journal of Church and State* 32 (1990), 501–9.

Prolingheuer, Hans. *Kirchenwende oder Wendekirche? Die EKD nach dem 9. November 1989 und ihre Vergangenheit.* Bonn: Pahl-Rugenstein, 1991.

BIBLIOGRAPHY

Ramet, Pedro. *Cross and Commissar: The Politics of Religion in Eastern Europe and the USSR.* Bloomington: Indiana University Press, 1987.

Rein, Gerhard. *Die protestantische Revolution, 1987-1990. Ein deutsches Lesebuch.* Berlin: Wichern, 1990.

Robinson, John A. T. *Honest to God.* London: SCM, 1963.

Röhm, Eberhard und Jörg Thierfelder. *Evangelische Kirche zwischen Kreuz und Hakenkreuz.* Stuttgart: Calwer, 1981.

Rumscheidt, Martin, ed. *Footnotes to a Theology: The Karl Barth Colloquium of 1972.* Corporation for the Publication of Academic Studies in Religion in Canada, 1974.

———. *Karl Barth in Re-View: Posthumous Works Reviewed and Assessed.* Pittsburgh: Pickwick, 1981.

———, ed. *The Way of Theology in Karl Barth: Essays and Comments.* Allison Park: Pickwick, 1986.

Sawatsky, Walter. "Truth-Telling in Eastern Europe: The Liberation and the Burden." *Journal of Church and State* 33 (1991) 701-29.

Scholder, Klaus. *The Churches and the Third Reich: Preliminary History and the Time of Illusions, 1918-1934.* Philadelphia: Fortress, 1988.

Schönherr, Albrecht. "Aufruhr des Gewissens. Der Kampf der Bekennenden Kirche in Deutschland zur Hitlerzeit." *Standpunkt* (1985) 16-21.

———. "A Contribution to the Direction of the Evangelical Church in the German Democratic Republic." *Occasional Papers on Religion in Eastern Europe* 7 (1987) 19-34.

Schönherr, Albrecht andWolf Krötke, eds. *Bonhoeffer-Studien. Beiträge zur Theologie und Wirkungsgeschichte Dietrich Bonhoeffers. Im Augtrage des Bonhoeffer-Komitees beim Bund der Evangelischen Kirchen in der DDR.* München: Chr. Kaiser, 1985.

Schottstädt, Bruno. "Christen und Kirchen in der DDR. Thesen." *Weißenseer Blätter* 4 (1982) 2-3.

Sievers, Hans-Jürgen. *Stundenbuch einer deutschen Revolution. Die Leipziger Kirchen im Oktober 1989.* Göttingen: Vandenhoeck & Ruprecht, 1990.

Sparn, Walter, ed. *Wieviel Religion braucht der deutsche Staat? Politisches Christentum zwischen Reaktion und Revolution.* Gütersloh: Gütersloher Verlagshaus Gerd Mohn, 1992.

Swoboda, Jörg, ed. *Die Revolution der Kerzen. Christen in den Umwälzungen der DDR.* Wuppertal: Oncken, 1990.

von Thadden, Rudolf. "Dietrich Bonhoeffer und die deutsche Nachkriegszeit (1945-1949)." *Kirchen in der Nachkriegszeit.* Göttingen: Vandenhoeck & Ruprecht, 1979.

Tschackert, Paul. "Art. Revolution, französische." *Realenzyklopädie für Theologie und Kirche* 16 (1905) 728.

Turner, Henry Ashby, Jr. *Germany from Partition to Reunification.* New Haven: Yale University Press, 1992.

———. *The Two Germanies since 1945.* New Haven: Yale University Press, 1987.

BIBLIOGRAPHY

Vellay, Rolf. "Kopf hoch!" *Weißenseer Blätter* 3 (1993) 38–39.
Weber, Hermann, ed. *DDR: Dokumente zur Geschichte der Deutschen Demokratischen Republik, 1945–1985*. München: Deutscher Taschenbuch, 1986.
———. *DDR. Grundriß der Geschichte, 1945–1990*. Hannover: Fackelträger, 1991.
———. *Geschichte der DDR*. München: Deutscher Taschenbuch, 1985.
West, Charles C. *Communism and the Theologians: Study of an Encounter*. New York: Macmillan, 1958.
Winter, Friedrich. "Öffentlich Schuld bekennen. Schuld und Vergebung vor und nach der 'Wende' im Bund der Evangelischen Kirchen (in der DDR)." *Kirchliche Zeitgeschichte* 4 (1991) 422–45.

Index

Adenauer, Konrad, 5, 33
Altizer, Thomas J. J., 25n15
Ananias, 57–58
Andersen, Hans Christian, 68
Ash, Timothy Garton, 7n10
Asmussen, Hans, 21n2

Bach, 60
Bark, Dennis L., 6n7
Barth, Karl, vii, viii, xi, 14, 19, 20n2, 21–23, 25–26, 41, 44, 44n3, 45, 60, 61n3, 64, 70–73, 77, 79, 80
Beethoven, 63
Beintker, Michael, vii, viii, ixn2–xn2, 33–34, 43–45, 47, 55
Besier, Gerhard, ixn1, 17n8
Bethge, Eberhard, 9n17, 24
Bonhoeffer, Dietrich, vii, 9, 13, 19, 23–26, 27, 41, 44, 45, 46n8
Bräcklin,, 17–18
Brandt, Willy, 5
Breipohl, Renate, 20n2
Brown, Robert McAfee, 61, 71n22
Bruesewitz, Oskar, ixn2, 10
Bultmann, Rudolf, 21
Burgess, John P., viii, 15, 16n6, 17n7
Busch, Eberhard, 21n3, 23

Cone, James H., 25n15
Currie, Jo Ann, viii

Day, Thomas I., 24–25, 25n14
DeGruchy, John W., 25n15
Dehn, Günter, 21
Dibelius, Martin, 55n22
Dibelius, Otto, 9, 29, 30n30, 54–55, 55n22

Elliger, Walter, 28
Engels, 32, 47, 51
Erhard, Ludwig, 5

Falcke, Heino, 14–16
Fessen, 29
Feuerbach, Ludwig, 48, 49n11
Franco, 34
Führer, Christian, xi

Gauck, Joachim, xi
Goeckel, Robert F., viii, ixn2, 7–9, 10, 11–12, 14–15, 16, 17–18, 36
Goethe, 60
Gogarten, Friedrich, 20n2, 21n2
Goldschmidt, Dieter, 31
Gorbachev, Mikhail, 6
Grabner, Jürgen, 7n10
Gress, Daivid R., 6n7
Grotewohl, Otto, 3, 4
Grüber, Heinrich, 26, 26n16
Gutierrez, Gustavo, 25n15
Gwertzman, Bernard, 7n10

INDEX

Hamel, Johannes, viii, x–xi, 14, 18, 45, 60–77, 78, 79, 80
Hamilton, William, 25n15
Hänisch, Günter, 6n8
Hans Meier. *See* Müller, Hanfried
Heinemann, 32
Heinze, Christiane, 7n10
Henry, David, xin5
Herpel, Otto, 21
Hindenburg, 35
Hitler, 23, 31, 35, 36
Holl, Karl, 21
Honecker, Erich, 5, 6, 10–11, 14, 31n33
Hunsinger, George, 23n12

Isaiah, 74
Iwand, Hans-Joachim, 26, 33, 44, 44n3

Jeremiah, 74–75
Jesus Christ, 37, 54, 63, 64, 65, 68, 69, 71, 73, 74

Kaufman, Michael T., 7n10
Kiesinger, Kurt, 5
Knittermeyer, Hinrich, 21n2
Kohl, Helmut, 6
Krummacher, Friedrich-Wilhelm, 16
Krusche, Werner, 16–17
Kullik, Second Lieutenant, 32
Kutter, Hermann, 20–21

Leith, John H., 36n46, 39n53, 41n59
Lenin, 25, 68
Lieb, Fritz, 21n2
Lilie, 29
Lilje, Hanns, 30n30
Linke, Dietmar, 26n16, 27–30
Luther, Martin, 11, 12, 21, 54, 60, 70

Marquardt, Friedrich-Wilhelm, 23n12
Marx, Karl, 31, 32, 47, 48, 49n11, 51

Merz, Georg, 20, 20n2
Mosse, George L., 9n15
Müller, Hanfried, vii, viii, x, 7, 13, 18, 19, 26–42, 44–59, 61, 76n35, 78, 79–80
Müller-Streisand, Rosemarie, vii, 27–28, 29, 32–33, 44

Naumann, Prorektor, 29
Niebuhr, Reinhold, 71, 76n35
Nielsen, Niels, 7n10
Niemöller, Martin, 32, 33, 44
Noth, Gottfried, 17–18

Paul, 75
Pilate, Pontius, 74
Pollack, Detlef, 7n10

Ragaz, Leonhard, 20–21
Reagan, Ronald, 5
Robespierre, 48
Robinson, John A. T., 25, 25n15
Roosevelt, Franklin D., 1

Sapphira, 57–58
Scharf, Kurt, 13
Schmidt, Helmut, 5
Schneider, 29–30
Schniewind, Julius, 60, 64
Scholder, Klaus, 19–20, 21
Schönherr, Albrecht, xn2, 9–10, 13–14, 17–18, 31n33
Schultheis, Heinrich, 21
Sgraja, 32
Sievers, Hans-Jürgen, 7n10
Stalin, 1
Stoecker, Adolf, 20n2
Stoph, Willi, 5
Strasser, 29
Stroup, John, viii, viiin1

Thurneysen, Eduard, 20n2–21n2, 73
Tillich, Paul, 20n2
Truman, Harry S, 1

Index

Turner, Henry Ashby, 3–4, 5n6, 6

Ulbricht, Walter, 2, 3, 4, 5

Vogel, 29

Wagner, Richard, 49n11

Weber, Hermann, 7n11
West, Charles, 60
Wolf, Ernst, 26
Wolf, Prof., 33
Wolf, Stephan, ixn1, 17n8

www.ingramcontent.com/pod-product-compliance
Lightning Source LLC
Chambersburg PA
CBHW070514090426
42735CB00012B/2775